MW01142720

Date Due

William E. Studwell
Dorothy E. Jones

Publishing Glad Tidings: Essays on Christmas Music

Publishing Glad Tidings: Essays on Christmas Music has been co-published simultaneously as *Music Reference Services Quarterly*, Volume 6, Number 4 1998.

Pre-publication
REVIEWS,
COMMENTARIES,
EVALUATIONS . . .

"**T**his is a fascinating compendium of Christmas carol trivia, but it is not trivial! Studwell knows more about this subject than any person alive. Whether your interest is casual or passionate, you'll find interesting facts, viewpoints, stories, and insights in this book–a reference work that will be invaluable for any reader who loves this most popular of musical forms."

Leonard Van Camp
Director of Choral Activities
Southern Illinois University
at Edwardsville

More pre-publication
REVIEWS, COMMENTARIES, EVALUATIONS . . .

"**F**or aficianados of Christmas carols, William E. Studwell again proves why he is considered one of the world's foremost authorities on this holiday genre. . . . *Publishing Glad Tidings: Essays on Christmas Music. . .* illuminates a territory upon which little light has been shed. . . . William Studwell and Dorothy Jones are right on the money!"

Ronald M. Clancy
CEO, Christmas Classics Ltd.
North Cape May, New Jersey

"**T**hese are thoughtful pieces on the collectors and translators who have enriched the Christmas musical tradition. I found this collection of essays to be interesting and informative."

C.T. Blickhan
Professor of Composition
and Coordinator of Graduate
Studies
School of Music
Northern Illinois University

Director of Music
First Congregational Church
of Christ
DeKalb, Illinois

The Haworth Press, Inc.

Publishing Glad Tidings: Essays on Christmas Music

Publishing Glad Tidings: Essays on Christmas Music has been co-published simultaneously as *Music Reference Services Quarterly*, Volume 6, Number 4 1998.

The *Music Reference Services Quarterly* Monographs/"Separates"

Foundations in Music Bibliography, edited by Richard D. Green

Minor Ballet Composers: Bibliographical Sketches of Sixty-Six Underappreciated Yet Significant Contributors to the Body of Western Ballet Music, edited by Bruce R. Schueneman and William E. Studwell

State Songs of the United States: An Annotated Anthology, edited by William E. Studwell and Bruce R. Schueneman

Publishing Glad Tidings: Essays on Christmas Music, by William E. Studwell and Dorothy E. Jones

These books were published simultaneously as special thematic issues of *Music Reference Services Quarterly* and are available bound separately. Visit Haworth's website at http: / /www.haworth.com to search our online catalog for complete tables of contents and ordering information for these and other publications. Or call 1-800-HAWORTH (outside US/Canada: 607-722-5857), Fax: 1-800-895-0582 (outside US/Canada: 607-771-0012), or e-mail getinfo @ haworth.com

Publishing Glad Tidings:
Essays on Christmas Music

William E. Studwell
Dorothy E. Jones

Dorothy E. Jones
Editor

Publishing Glad Tidings: Essays on Christmas Music has been co-published simultaneously as *Music Reference Services Quarterly*, Volume 6, Number 4 1998.

The Haworth Press, Inc.
New York • London

Publishing Glad Tidings: Essays on Christmas Music has been co-published as *Music Reference Services Quarterly,* Volume 6, Number 4 1998.

The development, preparation, and publication of this work has been undertaken with great care. However, the publisher, employees, editors, and agents of The Haworth Press and all imprints of The Haworth Press, Inc., including The Haworth Medical Press and Pharmaceutical Products Press, are not responsible for any errors contained herein or for consequences that may ensue from use of materials or information contained in this work. Opinions expressed by the author(s) are not necessarily those of The Haworth Press, Inc.

Cover design by Thomas J. Mayshock Jr.

The Haworth Press, Inc., 10 Alice Street, Binghamton, NY 13904-1580 USA

Library of Congress Cataloging-in-Publication Data

Studwell, William E. (William Emmett), 1936-
Publishing glad tidings : essays on Christmas music / William E. Studwell, Dorothy E. Jones ; Dorothy E. Jones, editor.
    p. cm.
    "Co-published simultaneously as Music reference services quarterly, volume 6, number 4 1998."
    Includes bibliographical references and index.
    ISBN 0-7890-0398-8 (alk. paper)
    1. Christmas music–History and criticism.   2. Carols–History and criticism.   3. Christmas music–Bio-bibliography.   4. Carols–Publishing–History.   5. Christmas music–Publishing–History. I. Jones, Dorothy E.   II. Music reference services quarterly.   III. Title.
ML2880.S8 1998   97-46983
782.28′1723–dc21   CIP
                                                                                                              MN

INDEXING & ABSTRACTING

Contributions to this publication are selectively indexed or abstracted in print, electronic, online, or CD-ROM version(s) of the reference tools and information services listed below. This list is current as of the copyright date of this publication. See the end of this section for additional notes.

- *CNPIEC Reference Guide: Chinese National Directory of Foreign Periodicals*, P.O. Box 88, Beijing, Peoples Republic of China

- *IBZ International Bibliography of Periodical Literature*, Zeller Verlag GmbH & Co., P.O.B. 1949, d-49009 Osnabruck, Germany

- *Information Science Abstracts*, Plenum Publishing Company, 233 Spring Street, New York, NY 10013-1578

- *Informed Librarian, The*, Infosources Publishing, 140 Norma Road, Teaneck, NJ 07666

- *International Index to Music Periodicals*, Chadwyck-Healey, Inc., 1101 King Street, Suite 380, Alexandria, VA 22314-2944

- *INTERNET ACCESS (& additional networks) Bulletin Board for Libraries ("BUBL"), coverage of information resources on INTERNET, JANET, and other networks.*
  - <URL:http://bubl.ac.uk/>
  - The new locations will be found under <URL:http://bubl.ac. uk/link/>.
  - Any existing BUBL users who have problems finding information on the new service should contact the BUBL help line by sending e-mail to <bubl@bubl.ac.uk>.
  The Andersonian Library, Curran Building, 101 St. James Road, Glasgow G4 ONS, Scotland

- *Library & Information Science Abstracts (LISA)*, Bowker-Saur Limited, Maypole House, Maypole Road, East Grinstead, West Sussex RH19 1HH, England

- *Library Literature*, The H.W. Wilson Company, 950 University Avenue, Bronx, NY 10452

(continued)

- *Music Index, The,* Harmonie Park Press, 23630 Pinewood, Warren, MI 48091

- *Newsletter of Library and Information Services,* China Sci-Tech Book Review, Library of Academia Sinica, 8 Kexueyuan Nanlu, Zhongguancun, Beijing 100080, People's Republic of China

- *RILM Abstracts of Music Literature,* City University of New York, 33 West 42nd Street, New York, NY 10036

SPECIAL BIBLIOGRAPHIC NOTES

*related to special journal issues (separates)
and indexing/abstracting*

☐ indexing/abstracting services in this list will also cover material in any "separate" that is co-published simultaneously with Haworth's special thematic journal issue or DocuSerial. Indexing/abstracting usually covers material at the article/chapter level.

☐ monographic co-editions are intended for either non-subscribers or libraries which intend to purchase a second copy for their circulating collections.

☐ monographic co-editions are reported to all jobbers/wholesalers/approval plans. The source journal is listed as the "series" to assist the prevention of duplicate purchasing in the same manner utilized for books-in-series.

☐ to facilitate user/access services all indexing/abstracting services are encouraged to utilize the co-indexing entry note indicated at the bottom of the first page of each article/chapter/contribution.

☐ this is intended to assist a library user of any reference tool (whether print, electronic, online, or CD-ROM) to locate the monographic version if the library has purchased this version but not a subscription to the source journal.

☐ individual articles/chapters in any Haworth publication are also available through the Haworth Document Delivery Service (HDDS).

Publishing Glad Tidings: Essays on Christmas Music

CONTENTS

∞　ALL HAWORTH BOOKS AND JOURNALS
　　ARE PRINTED ON CERTIFIED
　　ACID-FREE PAPER

William E. Studwell, MA, MSLS, is Professor and Principal Cataloger at the University Libraries of Northern Illinois University in DeKalb. The author of *The Americana Song Reader* (The Haworth Press, Inc., 1997), Mr. Studwell is the author of twelve other books on music including reference books on popular songs, state songs, ballet, and opera. He has also written three books on cataloging and over 300 articles on library science and music. A nationally known expert on carols, college fight songs, and Library of Congress subject headings, he has made over 300 radio, television, and print appearances in national, regional, and local media. Studwell is the Editor of *Music Reference Services Quarterly* (The Haworth Press, Inc.) and coauthor of the book *Minor Ballet Composers* (The Haworth Press, Inc., 1997).

Dorothy E. Jones, MRE, MLS, is Reference Librarian at Northern Illinois University in DeKalb, Illinois. She has earned degrees in religion and library science and studied music, organ, and conducting at a variety of institutions, including Duke University, Union Theological Seminary, and the University of California, Berkeley. An accomplished church chorus director and organist in both Illinois and California over the last 25 years, Dorothy is currently a private piano teacher as well as the organist for First Congregational United Church of Christ, DeKalb.

Preface

The Christmas carol is both a religious and cultural phenomenon, and an art form. Carol-singing has had its ups and downs in the course of a very long history. At times it seemed it might become one of the many important celebrative practices to disappear. However, from times of apathy or downright antagonism toward the joyous celebration of Christmas, there always emerged people who, because of religious, sociological, historical or musical interests, cared about the survival of the Christmas carol. These are individuals to whom we owe a great debt. They have observed long-term trends even as they participated in the small span of history in which their lives were lived. They collected Christmas carols from ancient manuscripts and from the memory-singing of mountain folk so that tunes and poems would not be lost. They wrote books to educate others and to create a pool of resources to help future researchers. These special people are the preservers and propagators of many carols which might have been lost but which are now available for performance, study and enjoyment. Mr. William Studwell, the editor of *Music Reference Services Quarterly* is a prolific present-day writer on the subject of the Christmas carol who also has many media presentations about Christmas carols to his credit. This collection of essays is a tribute to him and to his contribution toward the propagation and preservation of music which is a major ingredient of the Christmas celebrations of people all over the world.

Dorothy E. Jones

[Haworth co-indexing entry note]: "Preface." Co-published simultaneously in *Music Reference Services Quarterly* (The Haworth Press, Inc.) Vol. 6, No. 4, 1998, p. xiii; and: *Publishing Glad Tidings: Essays on Christmas Music* (William E. Studwell, and Dorothy E. Jones) The Haworth Press, Inc., 1998, p. xiii. Single or multiple copies of this article are available for a fee from The Haworth Document Delivery Service [1-800-342-9678, 9:00 a.m. - 5:00 p.m. (EST). E-mail address: getinfo@haworth.com].

xiii

PROPAGATORS
OF THE CHRISTMAS CAROL:
THE PIONEER COLLECTORS

Theodoric Petri,
Compiler of *Piae Cantiones*

William E. Studwell
Dorothy Jones

Although printing from movable type began to alter radically the world's civilization in the middle of the 15th century, it was, quite understandably, several decades before Christmas carols were printed. Carols then (as well as now) tended to be treated as minor cultural phenomena and therefore were pushed toward the back of the priority line. The first known printing of carols was in 1521, by an Englishman with the quaint and appropriate name Wynkyn de Worde. As an indicator that things really do not change that much despite the passage of centuries, the stated purpose for putting the set of carols onto paper was to provide "festival chansons for enlivening the Christmas celebrity." Only two carols from 1521 work have survived. One of these is the well known 15th-century rouser from Oxford University, "The Boar's Head Carol."

This first printing was completely logical. It occurred in the country which by far has contributed the most to the body of Christmas carols, and took place towards the beginning of the English Renaissance. Furthermore, the printing was done by an apprentice of and successor to the great pioneer printer William Caxton.

Much less logical was the appearance of the first important collection

This series of articles originally appeared in *The American Organist* Magazine between March 1991 and December 1994. The series is copyrighted by the American Guild of Organists and reprinted by permission.

[Haworth co-indexing entry note]: "Theodoric Petri, Compiler of *Piae Cantiones*." Studwell, William E., and Dorothy Jones. Co-published simultaneously in *Music Reference Services Quarterly* (The Haworth Press, Inc.) Vol. 6, No. 4, 1998, pp. 3-5; and: *Publishing Glad Tidings: Essays on Christmas Music* (William E. Studwell, and Dorothy E. Jones) The Haworth Press, Inc., 1998, pp. 3-5. Single or multiple copies of this article are available for a fee from The Haworth Document Delivery Service [1-800-342-9678, 9:00 a.m. - 5:00 p.m. (EST). E-mail address: getinfo@haworth.com].

of carols. In 1582, in then relatively remote Greifswald, Sweden, a book of about 200 pages was issued. Entitled *Piae Cantiones Ecclesiasticae et Scholasticae Veterum Episcoporum*, it was a collection of 73 Latin hymns and carols along with accompanying tunes. They were part-songs, for one to four voices, gathered from libraries in Germany, England, and France, and published for the use of Swedish Lutherans. On top of the international mix of Sweden, Germany, England, France, and by implication Italy (because of the Latin lyrics), one other country was also associated with *Piae Cantiones*.

The compiler of the volume was from Finland, an even more improbable geographical factor. By his preservation of these sacred songs then in vogue in Sweden and Finland, the Reverend Theodoric Petri of Nyland also preserved a small niche for himself in the history of western culture. Little is known about Petri except that he flourished around 1580 to 1625, and that he was also known under the names Didrik Petri, Theodoricus Petri (Rutha), and Theodore Peter Rhuta. The town he is linked with, Nyland, Finland, is also known as Nylandslän. Uusimaa, and Uudenmaanlääni. It appears that Petri was relatively young when he edited his famous volume.

A second edition of *Piae Cantiones* was published in Stockholm in 1616, translated into Finnish under the title *Wanhain Suomenmaan Pijspain*. A third edition was published at Rostock, Germany, in 1625, under the original title. Another reproduction of the original was issued in 1679. All this publication activity suggests that *Piae Cantiones* was relatively popular in Northern Europe for at least a century.

Yet when Thomas Helmore and John Mason Neale got their hands on a copy of the 1582 edition in the early 1850s, the volume was extremely rare. Quite possibly the copy, which was brought from Stockholm, was the only one left in existence. (Later editions, though, were still extant.) Helmore adapted the carol melodies and Neale either paraphrased the carol lyrics into English or wrote entirely new lines. Both music and words were published in *Carols for Christmas-tide* (London: J.A. Novello, 1853-54). Part two of this work was entitled *Carols for Easter-tide*.

Piae Cantiones, one of the jewels of the Renaissance, is notable because of its historical role as the first important compilation of Christmas carols. It predated by 240 years the next important carol collection, Davies Gilbert's 1822 *Some Ancient Christmas Carols*. It is also of interest for its printing of a certain anonymous 13th-century tune which when fitted with new lyrics by Neale in 1853 became one of the most beloved of holiday songs, *Good King Wenceslas*. So Petri's unique publication has contributed both to the continuum of history and to our present enjoyment of the winter holiday.

BIBLIOGRAPHY

The Oxford Book of Carols (London: Oxford University Press, 1964), p. ix.
John Julian, *A Dictionary of Hymnology* (New York: Dover, 1957), pp. 210-12.

Davies Gilbert, Compiler
of *Some Ancient Christmas Carols*

William E. Studwell
Dorothy Jones

In the late 19th century William Schwenck Gilbert and Arthur Sullivan won great and lasting fame as the illustrious Gilbert and Sullivan operetta team. In the early 19th century another G. and S. pair gained much less fame, but still endure, for their contributions to another genre of music. Davies Gilbert and William Sandys, two Englishmen who could not really be called musicians, in time became so closely associated with the Christmas carol in Great Britain that it almost seemed as if carols not linked with either man were socially inferior.

So many English carol books claimed to be derived from Gilbert and/or from Sandys that one might easily get the impression that the two men had gathered a virtual cornucopia of old folk carols. Yet the collections which brought them attention were not very extensive in content. Gilbert's first carol book contained only eight songs, with accompanying tunes. Sandys's first carol book was considerably larger, with 80 song texts, but only 18 tunes were printed. (Note the three numbers, eight, 80, and 18, all containing the number eight, which are associated with Gilbert and Sandys's collections from the 1800s.)

Although Gilbert's and Sandys' names are frequently linked, they worked independently and as far as is known never met each other. (A fuller sketch about Sandys will be given in the third artIcle in this series.)

Davies Gilbert (1767-1839) originally had the last name of Giddy but assumed his wife's surname Gilbert in 1817. He was educated at Pen-

---

[Haworth co-indexing entry note]: "Davies Gilbert, Compiler of *Some Ancient Christmas Carols*." Studwell, William E. and Dorothy Jones. Co-published simultaneously in *Music Reference Services Quarterly* (The Haworth Press, Inc.) Vol. 6, No. 4, 1998, pp. 7-10; and: *Publishing Glad Tidings: Essays on Christmas Music* (William E. Studwell, and Dorothy E. Jones) The Haworth Press, Inc., 1998, pp. 7-10. Single or multiple copies of this article are available for a fee from The Haworth Document Delivery Service [1-800-342-9678, 9:00 a.m. - 5:00 p.m. (EST). E-mail address: getinfo@haworth.com].

zance, a place which his later and more famous namesake magnificently immortalized in an operetta about pirates, and also at Pembroke College, Oxford. A country gentleman, Gilbert had an eclectic and busy career. In 1792-93, he was High Sheriff of Cornwall. In 1804 and from 1806 to 1832, he served in Parliament, where he promoted the arts and science. In 1820, he was treasurer of the Royal Society and from 1827 to 1830, its president.

Among his non-carol writings are:

- Collections and Translations Respecting St. Noet, and the Former State of His Church in Cornwall (1830);
- Memoir of Michael de Tregury, Archbishop of Dublin (1831);
- On Some Properties of the Catenarian Curve, with Reference to Bridges by Suspension (1821);
- On the Expediency of Assigning Specific Names to All Such Functions of Simple Elements as Represent Definite Physical Properties (1827);
- On the General Nature and Advantages of Wheels and Springs for Carriages (1825);
- On the Mathematical Theory of Suspension Bridges (1826);
- On the Nature of Negative and Imaginary Quantities (1831);
- On the Progressive Improvements Made in the Efficiency of Steam Engines in Cornwall (1830);
- On the Vibrations of Heavy Bodies in Cycloidal and in Circular Arches (1823);
- The Parochial History of Cornwall (1838); and
- A Plain Statement of the Bullion Question (1811).

He also edited two mystery plays from Cornwall. In summary, he was a well-educated, intelligent, and versatile person who competently dabbled in history, religion, economics, engineering, physics, and mathematics, as well as being a long-term politician.

The area which brought him the most notoriety was, of course, his compilation of Christmas carols. Although Gilbert was not in any sense of the word a true musician, he did possess enough musical ability to do a creditable job of carol editing. His first carol collection was *Some Ancient Christmas Carols, with the Tunes to Which They Were Formerly Sung in the West of England* (London: J. Nichols and Sons, 1822). The eight carols in this small 36-page, eleven-plate volume are:

- The Lord at First Did Adam Make,
- When God at First Created Man,

- A Virgin Most Pure,
- When Righteous Joseph Wedded Was,
- Hark! Hark! What News the Angels Bring,
- While Shepherds Watched their Flocks by Night,
- God's Dear Son Without Beginning, and
- Let All That Are to Mirth Inclined.

Note that only two of these songs, *A Virgin Most Pure* and *While Shepherds Watched*, are still utilized to much extent today, at least in the United States. Furthermore, the tune printed for *While Shepherds Watched* is not one with which the text has been commonly associated. (The hymn-like anonymous 1592 English tune which is often used was not linked with Nahum Tate's 1700 lyrics until 1861, and Handel's lively 1728 melody which is frequently used was not so linked until some unknown later time.)

No doubt responding to the immediate success of his first compilation, Gilbert came out with a second edition just one year later, in 1823. Issued by the sample publisher, the new version included eleven more carols, but without any more tunes, plus additional text, increasing the size of the second edition to a still modest 79-page, 20-plate volume. Only one of the eleven added carols, *The First Nowell*, is particularly familiar. The entire list is:

- The First Nowell,
- Augustus Caesar Having Brought,
- This New Christmas Carol,
- When Jesus Christ Was Twelve Years Old,
- In These Twelve Days,
- Zacharias Being an Aged Man,
- Now Carol We, and Carol We,
- Hark! All Around the Welkin Rings,
- Saint Stephen Was a Holy Man,
- When Bloody Herod Reigned King, and
- When Herod in Jerusalem.

To summarize Gilbert's Carol accomplishments, in his two editions he published only 18 carol texts plus eight melodies. Only three of the lyrics are still in the active U.S. holiday repertoire, and one of them, *A Virgin Most Pure*, is marginally popular. None of the tunes are commonly used today. So, in effect, if you evaluate his work from the viewpoint of current American popular culture, Gilbert only passed down to us the texts of *While Shepherds Watched Their Flocks* and *The First Nowell*.

But the key to understanding Gilbert's contributions to the history of carols lies not in the practical utility of his efforts to us today, but in the timing of his work. He compiled the first significant collection of English language Christmas carols. He was the pioneer. He was the apparent inspiration or model for a number of subsequent English carol collectors, adapters, and translators. His heirs include William Sandys, Thomas Helmore, John Mason Neale, Ramsden Bramley, John Stainer, and Richard Robert Chope.

These later carolists would all leave more to posterity, yet Gilbert ranks at least as high as the others simply because he started it all. After Gilbert's little landmark pamphlet appeared in 1822, interest in Christmas carols was strongly revived in England and elsewhere, and a long period of fruitful carol activity was set in motion. Aided by the enormous popularity of Dickens's classic 1843 tale, *A Christmas Carol*, the grand era of carol propagation extended at least 100 years, to *The Oxford Book of Carols* in 1928. It is even possible that Gilbert's resurrection of the carol also indirectly influenced Dickens in the creation of his holiday masterpiece.

As in the biblical parable, Gilbert planted a cultural mustard seed. Considering that his *Some Ancient Christmas Carols* was a relatively incidental aspect of his life and work, the legacy it left behind is remarkable.

BIBLIOGRAPHY

Julian, John. *A Dictionary of Hymnology*. New York: Dover, 1957, p. 211.
Terry, Richard R. *Gilbert and Sandys' Christmas Carols: With Six Collateral Tunes*. London: Burns Oates & Washbourne, 1931.

William Sandys,
Author of *Christmas Carols, Ancient and Modern*

William E. Studwell
Dorothy Jones

Take William Sandys plus Charles Dickens plus Williams Sandys and you have a dickens of a holiday sandwich. The first ingredient, bread slice one, was Sandys's 1833 book, *Christmas Carols, Ancient and Modern*. In that volume Sandys lamented that as a festive occasion, Christmas was on the decline in early 19th-century England:

> In many parts of the kingdom, especially in the northern and western parts, this festival is still kept up with spirit among the middling and lower classes, though its influence is on the wane even with them; the genius of the present age requires work and not play, and since the commencement of this century a great change may be traced. The modern instructors of mankind do not think it necessary to provide for popular amusements.

Sandys's observations were quite correct. As an immediate indirect by-product of the Industrial Revolution which had its initial manifestations a half century before, and as a lingering direct result of the suppression of secular Christmas celebrations during the Puritan Revolution of the mid-17th century, Christmas was clearly at a low point around the time Sandys made his complaint.

[Haworth co-indexing entry note]: "William Sandys, Author of *Christmas Carols, Ancient and Modern*." Studwell, William E., and Dorothy Jones. Co-published simultaneously in *Music Reference Services Quarterly* (The Haworth Press, Inc.) Vol. 6, No. 4, 1998, pp. 11-14; and: *Publishing Glad Tidings: Essays on Christmas Music* (William E. Studwell, and Dorothy E. Jones) The Haworth Press, Inc., 1998, pp. 11-14. Single or multiple copies of this article are available for a fee from The Haworth Document Delivery Service [1-800-342-9678, 9:00 a.m. - 5:00 p.m. (EST). E-mail address: getinfo@haworth.com].

But by 1833 there were signs that this negative trend was being reversed. In 1822 Davies Gilbert had published the first significant collection of English Christmas carols, *Some Ancient Christmas Carols*. In the very same year the American Clement Moore had written his famous poem, *A Visit from St. Nicholas*, giving a tremendous boost to the popular observance of Christmas in the United States. Add to these events Gilbert's issuance of a second edition of his carol compilation in 1823 and Sandys's 1833 volume about the holiday, and the groundwork for cultural reversal was firmly established.

The full revitalization of the December holiday in England was brought about by Charles Dickens's 1843 phenomenon of fiction, *A Christmas Carol*. In the Sandys-Dickens-Sandys sandwich, accordingly, Dickens was the meat, the most important part of the process. Despite his many fine writings on other themes, Dickens and Christmas became so closely intertwined in the hearts of his countrymen that his death in 1870 seemed to be a cruel blow to the holiday. But thanks to the vigorous movement that he and others like Sandys had given to the annual festivities, Christmas continued to flourish after Dickens.

The third ingredient in the figurative sandwich was Sandys's 1852 book, *Christmastide: Its History, Festivities, and Carols*. To some extent this was a continuation of the author's *Christmas Carols, Ancient and Modern*, and to some extent it was new material. The two Christmas volumes by Sandys surrounded by about a decade the classic by Dickens. One was a precursor to Dickens, and along with Gilbert's carol collection may have influenced the creation of *A Christmas Carol*. The other was a successor to Dickens, riding on the enormous success of his Christmas tale.

William Sandys, who in the flow of Christmas history can be mentioned without exaggeration in the same general context as the great Dickens, was a multifaceted person. A practicing London solicitor (lawyer) from 1814 to 1873, Sandys (1792-1874) was educated at Westminster. In addition to law and music, he dabbled in literature, language, and Freemasonry. Among his publications were:

- Festive Songs, Principally of the Sixteenth and Seventeenth Centuries (1848);
- The History of the Violin (1864);
- Shakespeare Illustrated by the Dialect of Cornwall (1847);
- A Short View of the History of Freemasonry (1829);
- Specimens of Cornish Provincial Dialect (1846);
- Specimens of Macaronic Poetry (1831); and
- Transactions of the Loggerville Literary Society [a satire] (1867).

His two most consequential works, the previously mentioned *Christmas Carols* and *Christmastide*, were, respectively, major and minor classics in the development of the Christmas carol. The 1833 work, with the full title *Christmas Carols, Ancient and Modern: Including the Most Popular in the West of England, with the Tunes to Which They Are Sung: Also Specimens of French Provincial Carols*, was published by R. Beckley in London. In size it was cxliv, 188 pages plus twelve plates of music. It contained the texts of 34 "ancient carols and Christmas songs from the early part of the 15th to the end of the 17th century," "a selection" of 40 "carols still used in the West of England," and six "French provincial" carols, plus 18 carol tunes, and extensive historical material and commentary.

Among the carols with tunes included in this historical volume were:

- A Virgin Most Pure;
- The First Nowell;
- God Rest You Merry, Gentlemen;
- To-morrow Shall Be My Dancing Day;
- I Saw Three Ships Come Sailing In; and
- Joseph Was an Old Man
  (Part 1 of the "Cherry Tree Carol").

Note that the refrain of *The First Nowell* as printed in Sandys varied considerably from the present melody. It was revised later in the century, possibly by Sir John Stainer. Also note that the tunes for "God Rest You Merry, Gentlemen" and "I Saw Three Ships" were not the melodies with which we are familiar today.

In summary, Sandys's *Christmas Carols* left us with the texts of 80 carols, including a half dozen still in the active U.S. repertoire, and 18 tunes, some of which are still in use. The most significant melodies preserved by Sandys were the ones for "The First Nowell" and "Tomorrow Shall Be My Dancing Day." Sandys also provided some valuable background material on the carol, particularly his description of the decline of the secular celebration of the Christmas holiday.

Sandys's later Christmas publication, *Christmastide: Its History, Festivities, and Carols*, was issued by John Russel Smith in London. It was not nearly as good a book as the earlier one, for two reasons. First, it was designed more for the popular market, that is, for the libraries of upper- and middle-class British families. While the 1833 volume leaned toward the scholarly, the 1852 volume tended to be of a general nature.

Second, it included fewer carols than its predecessor. The 80 carol texts and 18 carol tunes of the 1833 publication were reduced to 42 and twelve in the 1852 publication. Yet in spite of these shortcomings, *Christmastide* was a valuable item because it propagated the carols to a wide audience and also presented much historical material about the secular and sacred observance of Christmas, including background on carols. It perhaps was the most satisfactory general volume on Christmas in the 19th century.

So although his contributions to the literature of the holiday do not by any mode of thinking match those of Charles Dickens, William Sandys, as suggested earlier, does at least deserve to be discussed along with the literary master in the overall picture. For a person who was only a part-time historian and author, Sandys's writings on carols (and Christmas in general) are quite significant. For a person who as an amateur musician was not a particularly good one (Gilbert was superior), Sandys's contributions to the collection and preservation of carols was extensive and extremely important.

Sandys was not the first major propagator of the Christmas carol. But he was the greatest of the pioneer carolists, as well as the first person to be deeply involved in the perennial minor musical genre.

BIBLIOGRAPHY

1. John Julian, *A Dictionary of Hymnology.* New York: Dover, 1957, p. 210.
2. William E. Studwell, "A Dickens Tale: The Story of a Christmas Carol," *Journal of Church Music* 24, No. 10: 5-8 (Dec. 1982).
3. Richard R. Terry. *Gilbert and Sandys' Christmas Carols: With Six Collateral Tunes.* London: Burns Oates & Washburne, 1931.

PROPAGATORS
OF THE CHRISTMAS CAROL:
THE GREAT COLLECTORS,
ADAPTERS, AND TRANSLATORS

Thomas Helmore,
Music Editor of *Carols for Christmas-tide*

William E. Studwell
Dorothy Jones

There is nothing in Thomas Helmore's life that suggests he was particularly odd or eccentric, although musicians are frequently accused of such characteristics. The only factor that makes one suspect any significant psychological peculiarities is Helmore's close association with John Mason Neale in the 1850s. As a future article will clearly demonstrate, Neale was a person who was a lot more than a little strange.

On the other hand, there is plenty of information in the historical records to indicate that Helmore (1811-90) was a moderately notable English musician. He was far from a great figure, and might best be described as a relatively minor one. He falls in that sizable limbo between the really famous and the definitely obscure.

The son of a Congregational minister, he was born in Kidderminster, Worcestershire. Educated at Oxford, he received a BA in 1840 and an MA in 1845. Note that he did not graduate from college until age 29. This delay was apparently not due to health or academic ability, but most likely was caused by economics and/or family priorities. Before he completed his degree, he worked as a teacher in his father's day school at Stratford-on-Avon. Both his early teaching experience and his early training in his father's choir were clearly to shape his later activities. In 1840, he became an ordained Anglican priest (a break from his upbringing) and was appointed curate and vicar of St. Michael's in Litchfield in that year.

Two years later, in 1842, Helmore moved to St. Mark's College in

[Haworth co-indexing entry note]: "Thomas Helmore, Music Editor of *Carols for Christmas-tide*." Studwell, William E., and Dorothy Jones. Co-published simultaneously in *Music Reference Services Quarterly* (The Haworth Press, Inc.) Vol. 6, No. 4, 1998, pp. 17-19; and: *Publishing Glad Tidings: Essays on Christmas Music* (William E. Studwell, and Dorothy E. Jones) The Haworth Press, Inc., 1998, pp. 17-19. Single or multiple copies of this article are available for a fee from The Haworth Document Delivery Service [1-800-342-9678, 9:00 a.m. - 5:00 p.m. (EST). E-mail address: getinfo@haworth.com].

Chelsea as vice principal and precentor, and he stayed there until 1877. His prime task at St. Mark's, which was a church school teacher training institution, was to instruct students in the singing of the daily choral services at the college chapel. The ultimate purpose of this instruction was to make new teachers better suited to reform and upgrade the musical activities in local parishes throughout the country. Helmore did this assignment with considerable enthusiasm and much skill, and soon St. Mark's became famous for its music. As a direct result of his success at St. Mark's, he was appointed master of the choristers of the Chapel Royal in 1846.

Helmore gained even more attention as an avid advocate of the use of medieval plainsong in congregational singing. As a speaker and writer on plainsong, he was the leading authority on the topic. Among his publications on plainsong were:

- The Hymnal Noted (1851-54)
- A Manual of Plain Song (1849-50)
- Plain Song (1878)
- The Psalter Noted (1849).

He also contributed a significant essay on plainsong to the *Dictionary of Musical Terms* (1881).

Helmore's expertise in plainsong led to his association with John Mason Neale, another Anglican priest. Neale's interest in working with old Greek and Latin sacred lyrics meshed well with Helmore's background. The Helmore-Neale team produced three significant works. One of these was the above-mentioned *The Hymnal Noted*, which was a collection of plainsong melodies handled by Helmore, along with translations of the original, texts devised by Neale.

The other two were *Carols for Christmastide* (1853) and *Carols for Easter-tide* (1854), both published by J.A. Novello, London. *Carols for Easter-tide* was in reality part two of *Carols for Christmas-tide*. The material for these two collections came from *Piae Cantiones* (1582), edited by Theodoric Petri of Nyland, Finland (see the first article of this series for more on *Piae Cantiones* and Petri).

Carols for Christmas-tide was a monumental work in the history of carols. Helmore's skillful adaptation of the old medieval chants (plainsong) and Neale's dedications to providing paraphrases or new lyrics resulted in the first important English language carol collection after William Sandys's *Christmas Carols, Ancient and Modern* (1833) (see the third article of this series for more on Sandys). The best known of the carols in Helmore and Neale's landmark collection was "Good King Wenceslas."

In addition to being the music editor for the 1853 volume, Helmore was a major player in the strange drama of the composition of the great Advent carol, "O Come, O Come, Emmanuel." Supposedly the original Latin words of the song, "Veni Emmanuel," were from the twelfth century, and the music was from the twelfth or thirteenth century. Yet, there is no clear or direct proof for these alleged medieval origins. The oldest known printing of the words was in 1710, and the oldest known appearance of the melody was the fifteenth century, in the gray chronological area between medieval and modern, when a variant was used by Franciscan nuns as a processional for the dead.

No matter where the original text may have come from, Neale translated some Latin lines into "O Come, O Come, Emmanuel." The new lyrics were published in 1851. In 1854, Helmore adapted some presumably medieval music (one or more plainsongs), from an unspecified source, to serve as the melody for Neale's translation. Under this cloud of uncertainty, the famous international carol was born. With so much doubt and vagueness surrounding the creation of the song, it has been erroneously thought that Helmore actually composed an original melody.

One of the few aspects of the history of "O Come, O Come, Emmanuel" that is reasonably sure is that neither the original words nor the original Latin lyrics had any affiliation with holiday music until brought together as a carol in the 1850s. Even more certain is Helmore's vital role as the extractor of the music from the depths of obscurity, thus bringing to life one of the most beloved of carols, or what could be described as the "musical soul" of the Christmas season.

Thomas Helmore was not as important a propagator of the Christmas carol as various other persons, including his collaborator, Neale. Yet without him one of the landmark carol collections probably would not have appeared, and we most likely would not have either "Good King Wenceslas" or "O Come, O Come, Emmanuel" in our holiday repertoire.

BIBLIOGRAPHY

Companion to the Hymnal: A Handbook to the 1964 Methodist Hymnal. Nashville: Abingdon Press, 1970, pp. 569-70.

Julian, John. *A Dictionary of Hymnology.* New York: Dover, 1957, pp. 211-12.

The New Grove Dictionary of Music and Musicians, ed. Stanley Sadie. London: MacMillan, 1980, Vol. 8, p. 468.

Studwell, William E. "A Carol of Two Centuries: O Come, O Come, Emmanuel," *Journal of Church Music,* Vol. 28, No. 10 [Dec. 1986], pp. 10-11.

John Mason Neale, Controversial Carol Lyricist

William E. Studwell
Dorothy Jones

A recent reference work on hymns (*Companion to the Hymnal*, p. 626) noted that "A paradox concerning [John Mason] Neale's work is the lack of official English recognition given his achievement." Following that statement was the observation that the Russians and Americans, distant foreigners, had, in contrast, given him some honors. About 60 years after the early death of Neale, the *Oxford Book of Carols*, edited by three of Neale's English countrymen, did render a brief bit of unofficial appreciation to the 19th-century carolist. But as a whole, Neale remains relatively unapplauded in England in spite of significant, even monumental, achievements in the field of church music. Is this a case of "a prophet without honor in his own country?" Is it a case of "familiarity breeds contempt?" Or is it something else?

To some extent, the lack of attention to Dr. Neale stems from the nature of his work. Much of his activity involved translations, and as will be discussed later in this series (Catherine Winkworth and Theodore Baker), translators are typically relegated to the background. Furthermore, a good proportion of his most famous artistic products were carols, and the carol is generally regarded as a minor genre.

Yet to even a greater extent, Neale's status may be a direct by-product of his personal characteristics and the circumstances of some of his most notable accomplishments. Much about his life and work was odd, eccentric, and peculiar.

[Haworth co-indexing entry note]: "John Mason Neale, Controversial Carol Lyricist." Studwell, William E., and Dorothy Jones. Co-published simultaneously in *Music Reference Services Quarterly* (The Haworth Press, Inc.) Vol. 6, No. 4, 1998, pp. 21-25; and: *Publishing Glad Tidings: Essays on Christmas Music* (William E. Studwell, and Dorothy E. Jones) The Haworth Press, Inc., 1998, pp. 21-25. Single or multiple copies of this article are available for a fee from The Haworth Document Delivery Service [1-800-342-9678, 9:00 a.m. - 5:00 p.m. (EST). E-mail address: getinfo@haworth.com].

Neale (1818-66) was born in London, the only son of an Evangelical minister. A graduate of Trinity College, Cambridge, in 1840, he was ordained an Anglican priest in 1842, but because of Anglo-Catholic leanings and chronic ill health, he never was assigned to a parish. Instead, from 1846 to his death, he was warden of Sackvllle College, a home for old men in Sussex. (Two peculiarities emerge already.)

As a substitute for everyday priestly activities, Neale turned to a lifetime of research and publication, normally a choice that would not be particularly unusual. But true to form, Neale favored the esoteric disciplines of antiquarian studies and Greek and Latin hymns. (More leanings toward the eccentric become evident.) Among his many publications were:

- A History of the Holy Eastern Church (1847)
- Stories from the Heathen Mythology (1847)
- Ecclesiological Notes on the Isle of Man, Sutherland, and the Orkneys (1848)
- Few Words of Hope on the Present Crisis of the English Church (1849)
- Victories of the Saints (1850)
- Readings for the Aged (1850)
- Evenings at Sackville College (1851)
- Lectures on Church Difficulties (1851)
- Medieval Hymns and Sequences (1851)
- The Hymnal Noted (1851)
- Carols for Christmas-tide (1853)
- Carols for Easter-tide (1854)
- A Hand-book for Travellers in Portugal (1855)
- The Life and Times of Bishop Torry (1856)
- Medieval Preachers and Medieval Preaching (1857)
- A History of the So-Called Jansenist Church of Holland (1858)
- Hymns, Ancient and Modern (1859)
- A Commentary on the Psalms, from Primitive and Medieval Writers (1860)
- Hymns of the Eastern Church (1862)
- Essays on Liturgiology and Church History (1863)
- Hymns, Chiefly Medieval, on the Joys and Glories of Paradise (1865).

Neale obviously was talented and very hardworking, even driven. Although the range of topics he treated was broad (and could be regarded as another sign of eccentricity), he tended to focus on the old, the Greek, and the Latin, especially in the 1850s and 1860s. As alluded to above, his most noted and lasting work related to translations from Greek and Latin and/or the creation of carols. Among the non-carol hymns he translated were:

- All Glory, Laud, and Honor
- Come, Ye Faithful, Raise the Strain
- Creator of the Stars of Night
- The Day of Resurrection
- Jerusalem the Golden.

The carols with which he was involved included:

- Angelus emittur (anonymous [late medieval?] hymn translated by Neale as "Gabriel's Message")
- Conditor aims siderum (anonymous seventh-century hymn translated by Neale as "Creator of the Stars of Night")
- Gongaudeat turba fidelium (anonymous eleventh-century hymn translated by Neale as "From Church to Church")
- Corde natus ex Parentis (early fifth-century Spanish hymn by Aurelius Clemens Prudentius, translated by Neale as "Of the Father's Love Begotten")
- Dies est leticiae (anonymous medieval hymn translated by Neale as "Royal Day That Chaseth Gloom")
- Good Christian Men, Rejoice (1853 free paraphrase of the anonymous 14th-century German carol "In dulci jubilo," attached to the original tune)
- Good King Wenceslas (original 1853 lyrics by Neale, attached to a anonymous 13th-century tune)
- Jesus' Bloemhof (15th-century Dutch folk carol translated by Neale as "Our Master Hath a Garden")
- Resonet in laudibus (anonymous 13th-or 14th-century German hymn translated by Neale as "Christ Was Born on Christmas Day")
- Veni, Emmanuel (anonymous [twelfth-century?] hymn translated by Neale as "O Come, O Come, Emmanuel")
- Veni, Redemptor gentium (late fourth-century Italian hymn by St. Ambrose, translated by Neale as "Come, Thou Redeemer of the Earth").

This list of carols is quite impressive, and along with his 1853 collection *Carols for Christmas-tide*, is a proper tribute to Neale's energy and devotion to the Christmas carol. However, if you examine more closely the background of the three famous carols he helped bring to the world, Neale's penchant toward the peculiar again leaps out.

"Good Christian Men, Rejoice," touted as a "new" song, was essentially pirated from "In dulci jubilo." The original song, furthermore, was by legend created after a session of singing and dancing with angels.

"Good King Wenceslas" is an idiosyncratic blend of a lively and most delightful melody with a set of rather horrible lyrics by Neale. The words have even been described as "doggerel." This is a clear case of the melody keeping the carol alive, although perhaps the clumsiness and strangeness of the lyrics have evoked a sort of perverse appeal. In other words, Neale's questionable poetry may have touched off the appetite for the odd and offbeat which is present in all of us

The history of "O Come, O Come, Emmanuel," which supposedly involved a normal translation, is full of curious sidelights. First, there is no real proof that the words and music of this great carol are from around the twelfth century as alleged. The circumstances of Neale's translation and the adaptation of the music by Thomas Helmore are quite fuzzy, causing some to suspect original composition by Neale and Helmore. Second, the song did not become a carol until the 1850s in spite of the reputed medieval origins of its ingredients. Third, some of the stanzas of Neale's translation are usually replaced by stanzas from a translation by Henry Sloane Coffin (1877-1954). (For more on this carol and on Helmore, Neale's collaborator on *Carols for Christmas-tide*, see the previous article in this series.)

The enduring reputation of Reverend John Mason Neale rests on his three renowned Christmas carols and his Easter song, "The Day of Resurrection." Despite his long litany of other achievements, he must primarily be judged by these four pieces. "Resurrection" is one of the finest hymns of the Easter season, and the three Christmas songs are in like manner towards the top of that holiday's music. Yet with the troubles and oddities associated with Neale's big three of Christmas, plus his general life pattern, it is understandable why the English have been reluctant to give him high honors. His extensive contributions to the propagation of the Christmas carol are duly acknowledged, but so is the somewhat tainted or at least eccentric environment persistently lingering all around him.

BIBLIOGRAPHY

Companion to the Hymnal: A Handbook to the 1964 Methodist Hymnal. Nashville: Abingdon Press, 1970, pp. 569-70.

Hatfield, Edwin F. *The Poets of the Church.* Boston: Milfold House, 1972, pp. 454-57.

Julian, John. *A Dictionary of Hymnology.* New York: Dover, 1957, pp. 211-12.
Studwell, William E. "A Carol of Two Centuries: O Come, O Come, Emmauel."
Journal of Church Music, Vol. 28, No. 10 (Dec. 1988), pp. 10-11.
_____. *Christmas Carols: A Reference Guide.* New York: Garland, 1985.
The Oxford Book of Carols. London: Oxford University Press, 1964. p. xxi.

Henry Ramsden Bramley, Lyrics Editor of *Christmas Carols, New and Old*

William E. Studwell
Dorothy Jones

From one perspective, Henry Ramsden Bramley was only a historical footnote to the work of the famous English musician, Sir John Stainer. But on the single important occasion when their divergent paths crossed, the legacy for which Bramley is partially responsible is so crucial in the history of the Christmas carol that he deserves some special attention.

The Reverend Henry Ramsden Bramley (1833-1917) was not very productive in activities which could be utilized by posterity. Prominent in his own time, including long-term Vicar of Horspath, Oxon, and for a while Dean of Magdalen College, Oxford, he did only a small amount of writing and editing for publication. Outside of the landmark carol collection on which he collaborated with John Stainer, and some hymns, his total known published work consists of:

- An Answer to Professor Goldwin Smith's Plea for the Abolition of Tests in the University of Oxford (1864)
- How Did S. Chrysostom Understand [Greek title]?: A Second Letter to the Reverend the Regius Professor of Divinity (1879)
- The Psalter, or Psalms of David and Certain Canticles [edited by Bramley] (1884)
- Some Remarks on the Debate in Congregation upon the Proposed Endowment of the Regius Professorship of Greek (1864)

[Haworth co-indexing entry note]: "Henry Ramsden Bramley, Lyrics Editor of *Christmas Carols, New and Old*." Studwell, William E., and Dorothy Jones. Co-published simultaneously in *Music Reference Services Quarterly* (The Haworth Press, Inc.) Vol. 6, No. 4, 1998, pp. 27-29; and: *Publishing Glad Tidings: Essays on Christmas Music* (William E. Studwell, and Dorothy E. Jones) The Haworth Press, Inc., 1998, pp. 27-29. Single or multiple copies of this article are available for a fee from The Haworth Document Delivery Service [1-800-342-9678, 9:00 a.m. - 5:00 p.m. (EST). E-mail address: getinfo@haworth.com].

Bramley's contributions to hymns were similarly meager. Perhaps the only two of his songs worth mentioning are the obscure carol, "The Great God of Heaven Is Come Down to Earth," which was included in *The English Hymnal* (1906), and "A Cradle Song of the Blessed Virgin," an 1871 carol found in a few carol books. If his reputation were based on his compositions or the four publications listed above, Bramley would today be a near nonentity.

Magdalen College was the key to Bramley's fame. While there he became acquainted with John Stainer who was appointed organist at the college in 1860. When the younger Stainer was granted his doctorate in 1865, Bramley was one of the persons who presented Stainer with his doctor's robes. From this friendship came the monumental collaboration between Bramley and Stainer. In 1871, Bramley, as editor of the words, and Stainer, as music editor, issued *Christmas Carols, New and Old* (London, Novello). With attractive engraved illustrations by the brothers Dalziel, and 42 carols with tunes, the collection and its subsequent expanded version were published in many editions, including ones well into the 20th century (1923, 1947, and 1950).

The 1871 edition consisted of two series or parts, the first series having 20 carols and the second 22. A third series was added in a later edition published around 1878. With the additional 28 carols with tunes in part three, the enlarged edition had a total of 70 carol texts with accompanying melodies, at the time a stupendous amount. The combination of many carols, impressive illustrative matter, a well-done preface, the novelty of an index providing the sources of the words and music, and competent, tasteful poetry and arrangements made Bramley and Stainer's carol book a big artistic and commercial success. It was both a volume of great importance to the history of carols and a tremendous hit with the British public. Of 19th-century compilers, only R.R. Chope with his *Carols for Use in Church* had more songs (112 in the 1875 edition; 215, counting carols for Easter and other seasons, in the 1894 edition).

But Chope's collections were not as well crafted and were not nearly as well received by the public. In the matter of quantity, no one came near to matching the efforts of Chope. In the matter of quality, Bramley and Stainer were probably first. When this excellence was coupled with the amount of carols compiled, adapted, translated, and arranged, especially in the later edition, Bramley and Stainer were clearly the class of the 19th-century carol propagators.

Note that in this essay, as well as in other places, Bramley's name is mentioned before Stainer's. Although Stainer is far better known and much more accomplished, Bramley should be given equal credit for their outstanding carol editions. If a guess had to be made, it was probably the more energetic Stainer who proposed the concept, and therefore Bramley in one sense could be regarded as the adjacent or secondary person in the project. Yet his contributions were as important as Stainer's, and most vitally, the blend of the talents of the two men produced an exceptional body of carols which have greatly enhanced the edification and enjoyment of the Christmas holiday.

BIBLIOGRAPHY

Chulton, Peter. *John Stainer and the Musical Life of Victorian Britain.* Newton Abbot: David & Charles, 1984, pp. 27, 137.

Julian, John. *A Dictionary of Hymnology.* New York: Dover, 1957, pp. 212-13, 1615.

Studwell, William E. *Christmas Carols: A Reference Guide.* New York: Garland, 1985, pp. xiv, xxviii, 5.

John Stainer, Music Editor
of *Christmas Carols, New and Old*

William E. Studwell
Dorothy Jones

For his many contributions to British music, John Stainer (1840-1901) was knighted by Queen Victoria in 1888. He was also honored by a full biography nearly a century after his death. Such attention for musicians is normally given only to highly successful composers and extraordinary performers, yet Stainer was neither. He composed about 150 hymn tunes, six cantatas and oratorios, eight services (full, evening, and communion), and other religious works. Today, though, only two of his works are commonly used, the 1887 oratorio *The Crucifixion* and the "Sevenfold Amen" (1873). The latter is very familiar to church congregations but is also very short. In addition, it was derived or arranged from the Dresden Amen.

Generally regarded as only a marginal composer, Stainer has received the most acclaim for his musicological activities. The son of a schoolmaster, he was introduced to church music at an early age. At seven he became a probationary member of the choir at St. Paul's Cathedral, and after a while became one of the soloists. At 14, he attained the first of his several positions as organist, including ones at Magdalen College, Oxford, in 1860, for the whole university in 1861, and at St. Paul's Cathedral in 1872. He was educated at Christ Church, Oxford, and received his doctorate in music in 1865.

His appointment at St. Paul's was perhaps the key event in his life. Stainer successfully pushed for long overdue music reforms at the cathe-

[Haworth co-indexing entry note]: "John Stainer, Music Editor of *Christmas Carols, New and Old.*" Studwell, William E., and Dorothy Jones. Co-published simultaneously in *Music Reference Services Quarterly* (The Haworth Press, Inc.) Vol. 6, No. 4, 1998, pp. 31-33; and: *Publishing Glad Tidings: Essays on Christmas Music* (William E. Studwell, and Dorothy E. Jones) The Haworth Press, Inc., 1998, pp. 31-33. Single or multiple copies of this article are available for a fee from The Haworth Document Delivery Service [1-800-342-9678, 9:00 a.m. - 5:00 p.m. (EST). E-mail address: getinfo@haworth.com].

dral, and soon became a very prominent and respected church musician. In 1874, he was a founder of the Musical Association. In 1889, he became professor of music at Oxford. In addition, he was president of the Musical Association, the Plainsong and Mediaeval Music Society, and the London Gregorian Society, and vice president of the Royal College of Organists. He also was author, co-author, editor, or co-editor of a variety of publications, including:

- The Cathedral Prayer Book (1891)
- The Cathedral Psalter (1874)
- Catalogue of English Song Books Forming a Portion of the Library of Sir John Stainer (1891)
- Choral Society Vocalisation (1895)
- Christmas Carols, New and Old (1871; expanded edition around 1878)
- The Church Hymnary (1898)
- Composition (1880)
- A Dictionary of Musical Terms (1876)
- Early Bodleian Music (1901)
- Harmony (1877)
- Music in Its Relations to the Intellect and the Emotions (1892)
- The Music of the Bible (1879)
- The Organ (1877)
- A Theory of Harmony Founded on the Tempered Scale (1871)

One of the more important publishing activities by Stainer was his collaboration with Henry Ramsden Bramley on *Christmas Carols, New and Old*. Bramley edited the words, and Stainer the music. The initial 1871 edition of 42 carols with tunes and the subsequent circa 1878 edition of 70 carols with tunes were both landmarks in the history of Christmas carols. The combination of a large number of songs along with excellent treatment of the words and music made the collections not only huge commercial successes but also set them clearly above other English language carol compilations of the 19th century.

Although Stainer did not write any carol melodies which are widely used, he may well have been instrumental in the development of one of the greatest of Christmas songs, "The First Nowell." When first printed by William Sandys in his *Christmas Carols, Ancient and Modern* (1833), the melody for the 16th-century favorite varied somewhat from the present version. The final line of the refrain ("Born is the King of Israel") was completely different, and other differences were also present. Under the music editorship of Stainer, the earlier form of the tune was rearranged to the current familiar form for the 1871 edition. One suspects that Stainer was directly responsible for the changes, having been influenced by an 1860 book, *Christmas: Its Customs and Carols*, by William Fyfe. In that volume was an anonymous carol entitled "The First Noel." Mostly dissimilar to the famous carol, the 1860 song did have a refrain similar to the present version. Stainer most likely extracted that superior section of "The First Noel," adapted it to "The First Nowell," and did some other arranging.

Stainer also may have contributed to the success of another quite significant carol, William Chatterton Dix's "What Child Is This?" Dix wrote the lyrics around 1865, and the song appeared in Bramley and Stainer attached to the marvelous 16th-century English folk melody, "Greensleeves." Stainer, who made a harmonization of the music for the 1871 edition, was quite possibly the individual who actually brought together the lyrics and the tune.

If the presumptions about Stainer's handling of "The First Nowell" and "What Child Is This?" are correct, then Stainer must be regarded as one of the very top propagators of the Christmas carol. Not only was he jointly responsible for the best and most popular carol collection of the 19th century, but he also helped breathe life into two of the favorites of our holiday music. While really not much of an original composer, Sir John Stainer was definitely first rate when it came to working with carols.

BIBLIOGRAPHY

Charlton, Peter. *John Stainer and the Musical Life of Victorian Britain*. Newton Abbot: David & Charles, 1984.
Companion to the Hymnal: A Handbook to the 1964 Methodist Hymnal. Nashville: Abingdon Press, 1970, pp. 668-69.
Julian, John. *A Dictionary of Hymnology*. New York: Dover, 1957, pp. 212-13.
The New Grove Dictionary of Music and Musicians, ed. Stanley Sadie. London: Macmillan, 1980, Vol. 18, pp. 57-58.
Studwell, William E. "The First Nowell: Some Historical and Critical Notes," *The American Organist*, Vol. 24, No. 2 (Feb. 1990), p. 88.

Richard Robert Chope,
Compiler of *Carols for Use in Church*

William E. Studwell
Dorothy Jones

Richard Robert Chope, compiler of the most voluminous English-language carol collection of the 19th century, completed a carol gathering process which began in 1822 with Davies Gilbert. Between the pioneer Gilbert and the quantitative champion Chope was a variety of other collectors, major and minor. The major collectors, William Sandys, Thomas Helmore with John Mason Neale, and Henry Ramsden Bramley with John Stainer, have been covered previously in this series.

Several lesser collectors are worth noting to get a better overall portrait of carol activity in 19th-century England. There were quite a few other persons who compiled carols, often anonymously, or who inserted carols in a book, but the five below are perhaps the most important or interesting:

Thomas Wright, compiler of *Songs and Carols* (1847)

Wright gathered songs from manuscripts in the British Museum.

William Henry Husk, compiler of *Songs of the Nativity* (1855)

Husk's substantial volume included many carol texts, but only twelve tunes.

William Wallace Fyfe, author of *Christmas, Its Customs and Carols* (1860)

Fyfe wrote an interesting volume on the holiday which included some

[Haworth co-indexing entry note]: "Richard Robert Chope, Compiler of *Carols for Use in Church*." Studwell, William E., and Dorothy Jones. Co-published simultaneously in *Music Reference Services Quarterly* (The Haworth Press, Inc.) Vol. 6, No. 4, 1998, pp. 35-38; and: *Publishing Glad Tidings: Essays on Christmas Music* (William E. Studwell, and Dorothy E. Jones) The Haworth Press, Inc., 1998, pp. 35-38. Single or multiple copies of this article are available for a fee from The Haworth Document Delivery Service [1-800-342-9678, 9:00 a.m. - 5:00 p.m. (EST). E-mail address: getinfo@haworth.com].

carols. One of the songs was "Fyfe's Noel," or "The First Noel," a folk carol whose refrain was probably the inspiration for an alteration to the refrain of the first published version of "The First Nowell" (1833), thereby creating the present (1870s) version of the great carol.

Edmund Sedding, compiler of *Ancient Christmas Carols* (1860)

Sedding only published nine carols, but among them was "Masters in This Hall," printed for the first time. Sedding himself discovered the lively tune at Chartres Cathedral in France, and asked his associate William Morris to write some lyrics for the 1860 collection.

Joshua Sylvester, compiler of *A Garland of Christmas Carols, Ancient and Modern* (1861)

Sylvester's compilation was one of the better collections prior to Bramley and Stainer's 1871 edition.

A definite contrast to these relatively minor figures was the Reverend R.R. Chope (1830-?), who was the most ambitious of all the 19th-century English carol collectors. Chope, in fact, was triply ambitious—chronologically because he dealt with carols for at least 37 years, from 1857 to 1894; versatilely because he not only handled Christmas carols but also songs for Epiphany, Easter, Ascension, and Harvest; and quantitatively because he compiled more than all of his predecessors.

A clergyman and musician educated at Exeter College, Oxford, and, from 1865, vicar of St. Augustine's in South Kensington, Chope quietly preserved for himself a little corner of cultural history by issuing five significant publications:

The Congregational Hymn & Tune Book (1857)

A collection of 138 hymns which included the first widely distributed printing of "Hark! The Herald Angels Sing" after Charles Wesley's 1739 text and Felix Mendelssohn's 1840 tune were brought together by English organist William Hayman Cummings in 1855. An enlarged second edition (1862) had 300 hymns.

Versicles, Canticles, Litany, & C.: The Prayer Book Noted & Pointed Throughout All Its Services (1862)

A small liturgical volume apparently to be used with Chope's hymnbook.

Carols for Use in Church During Christmas and Epiphany (1875)

Published by Metzler & Co., London, this large compilation included 112 carols with tunes. The music was edited by Herbert Stephen Irons and an introduction was written by Sabine Baring-Gould. Baring-Gould is best known as the lyricist for the hymn "Onward, Christian Soldiers," but he also provided the words for three moderately well-known Christmas carols, "Gabriel's Message," "The Infant King," and "Sleep, My Saviour, Sleep." (Note that another carol, "Angelus emittur," was translated by John Mason Neale using the title "Gabriel's Message.") The collection was also known under the title, *Carols, Ancient and Modern, Words and Music, for Use in Church During Christmas and Epiphany.* The earlier versions of this publication may date back as far as 1868.

Carols for Easter and Other Tides (1887)

This may or may not be essentially the same as another title, *Easter and Harvest Carols* (1884).

Carols for Use in Church During Christmas and Epiphany, Easter, Ascension, and Harvest (1894)

Published by W. Clowes & Sons, London, this huge compilation included 215 carols with tunes, mostly for Christmas and Epiphany. It is an expanded version of the 1875 carol collection, plus the addition of material from Chope's 1887 Easter and other tides collection. Irons was once again the chief music editor, and Baring-Gould's introduction again appears.

Add to these his being the longtime assistant editor of the periodical, *Literary Churchman*, and one of the originators of another periodical, *The Choir and Musical Record*, and the career of Chope could be characterized as double-pronged. His two-edition hymnbook and his little 1862 liturgical book, along with other activities, put him at the forefront of the revival and reform of church music in England.

Most importantly, because of his big 1875 carol compilation and his even bigger 1894 clustering of carols, all with music, Chope was a leading propagator of the Christmas carol. He definitely was not the first, and surely was not the best, but for sheer volume, for mass dissemination to the general public, no one in the 19th century matched Richard Robert Chope.

BIBLIOGRAPHY

Julian, John. *A Dictionary of Hymnology.* New York: Dover, 1975. pp. 208-13, 223-24.

Studwell, William E. *Christmas Carols: A Reference Guide.* New York: Garland, 1985, pp. xv, xix.

_____. "Glory to the New-born King," *Journal of Church Music*, Vol. 21. No. 10 (Dec. 1979), p. 4.

_____, and Dorothy Jones, "Obscure Carol Classics: Charles Hutchins' Carols Old and Carols New," *The Choral Journal*, Vol. 29. No. 1 (August 1988), p. 11.

Catherine Winkworth
and Theodore Baker:
Translators Extraordinary

William E. Studwell
Dorothy Jones

Translators seldom receive a large amount of attention in our culture. One indicator of the almost invisible status of such linguists is a longstanding cataloging policy of the Library of Congress. For years, the most influential library in the world has in most cases not made translators a library catalog access point. That is, users of libraries usually cannot find a book by looking under the name of the translator.

Similarly, translators for politicians and other leaders tend to be anonymous. On rare occasions, the faces of translators associated with famous persons may become familiar to the public. In the 1980s and 1990s, the male translator who was a constant companion of Mikhail Gorbachev whenever he was interacting with the United States became somewhat of a nameless celebrity. Yet, as a whole, translators are an underappreciated and more or less forgotten group. Some translators, Henry Wadsworth Longfellow for instance, have become very famous, but their renown came in activities other than their linguistic accomplishments.

There are exceptions, though. A prominent example of a person gaining much attention by means of translation work is Catherine Winkworth. London-born Winkworth (1827-78) devoted the middle part of her life to translating sacred songs from the German. Her most noted achievement was the book *Lyra Germanica: Hymns for the Sundays and Chief Festivals*

[Haworth co-indexing entry note]: "Catherine Winkworth and Theodore Baker: Translators Extraordinary." Studwell, William E., and Dorothy Jones. Co-published simultaneously in *Music Reference Services Quarterly* (The Haworth Press, Inc.) Vol. 6, No. 4, 1998, pp. 39-42; and: *Publishing Glad Tidings: Essays on Christmas Music* (William E. Studwell, and Dorothy E. Jones) The Haworth Press, Inc., 1998, pp. 39-42. Single or multiple copies of this article are available for a fee from The Haworth Document Delivery Service [1-800-342-9678, 9:00 a.m. - 5:00 p.m. (EST). E-mail address: getinfo@haworth.com].

of the Christian Year (1855). *Lyra* contained 103 translations of German hymns gathered from an 1833 collection, *Versuch eines allgemeinen Gesang und Gebetbuchs*, compiled by Christian Karl Josias Bunsen.

Lyra Germanica was published in a number of editions and its considerable success led to a somewhat less important second series. *Lyra Germanica: Second Series: The Christian Life* was first issued in 1858 and like its predecessor had multiple printings. The second series, selected from various sources but mostly from Bunsen's 1833 collection once again, included 123 hymn translations. One of the editions of the *Lyra* appeared in 1862 under the title *The Chorale Book for England*. Other editions had the titles *Songs for the Household and Songs, Sacred and Devotional*.

Winkworth also translated two biographies, Emma Poel's *Life of Amelia Wilhelmina Sieveking* (1863) and the *Life of Pastor Fliedner of Kaiserswerth* (1867). She also wrote a history of German hymns, *Christian Singers of Germany* (1869), which had multiple editions. Incidentally, her older sister, Susanne Winkworth (1820-84), was also a translator of note.

Among the translations in the *Lyra* were several well-known or enduring Christmas carols, namely:

- Fröhlich soll mein Herze springen (1653 lyrics by Paul Gerhardt, translated as "All My Heart This Night Rejoices");
- Macht hoch die Tür, die Tor' mach heit (1642 lyrics by Georg Weissel, translated as "Lift Up Your Heads, Ye Mighty Gates");
- Tröstet, tröstet, meine Leben (1671 lyrics by Johann Olearius, translated as "Comfort, Comfort Ye My People");
- Vom Himmel hoch, da komm ich her (1535 lyrics by Martin Luther, translated as "From Heaven Above to Earth I Come");
- Wachet auf! Ruft uns die Stimme (1599 lyrics by Philipp Nicolai, translated as "Wake, Awake, for Night Is Flying");
- Wie schön leuchtet der Morgenstern (1599 lyrics by Philipp Nicolai, translated *twice* as "How Brightly Beams the Morning Star" and "O Morning Star, How Fair and Bright").

Especially because of her English renderings of four top carols (the ones by Luther, Gerhardt, and Nicolai), Winkworth could be categorized as the greatest carol translator ever. In effect, she introduced the English-speaking world to roughly half of the more familiar and popular German language carols. (While some of the four renowned carols had other translations, Winkworth's dominated in every instance.) No other person has linguistically converted as many leading carols, and few have done it with as much skill.

Not very far behind Winkworth in the art of carol translation was American Theodore Baker (1851-1934). He was responsible for the most used English versions of these famous carols, two German, and one Italian. His linguistic mini-masterpieces were:

- Als ich bei meinen Schafen wacht (16th-century folk lyrics from Germany, translated as "While by My Sheep I Watch at Night," also known as "Echo Carol");
- Canzone di zampognari (possibly 17th-century folk lyrics from Sicily, translated as "Carol of the Bagpipers");
- Es ist ein' Ros' entsprungen (15th-century folk lyrics from Germany, translated as "Lo, How a Rose E'er Blooming").

Note that between them, Winkworth and Baker almost cornered the market in translations of prominent German Christmas songs. The only other German-language carols of equal or greater fame which were not handled by Winkworth or Baker were "Stille Nacht, heilige Nacht" (converted to "Silent Night, Holy Night" by John Freeman Young [1820-85]) and "O Tannenbaum" (with various translations, most usually "O Christmas Tree").

But in spite of their mutual focus on German carols, Winkworth and Baker were in several ways different. Baker also tried Italian, providing a very good lyric for the leading carol from Italy. In addition, Baker dealt solely with the folk idiom in contrast with Winkworth's preoccupation with mainstream hymns. And while Winkworth is primarily known for her translations, the main thrust of Baker's work lies elsewhere.

Although he prepared a large number of translations for German-language musicological books, he is best known for his outstanding scholarly reference work, *Baker's Biographical Dictionary of Musicians*. First published in 1900, the dictionary has gone through several editions, the most recent ones edited by Nicolas Slonimsky. No other single-volume English-language work provides more data on figures in the field of music. Only the multi-volume *Grove's Dictionary* (in its various editions) provides a larger amount of reliable biographical information.

Baker also published a *Dictionary of Musical Terms* (1895) and a *Pronouncing Pocket Manual of Musical Terms* (1905). Baker was both a very accomplished musicologist and an artful translator of carols. In the compilation of biographical material on musicians, he was perhaps second only to Sir George Grove. In the translation of famous Christmas songs, he was second only to Catherine Winkworth. (A good argument, even, could be made for Baker being slightly superior to Winkworth.)

Both Winkworth and Baker had significant roles in the development of the Christmas carol. Jointly, the lucky seven songs of renown which they helped propagate are an appreciable part of our contemporary musical celebration of the holiday season.

BIBLIOGRAPHY

Grove's Dictionary of Music and Musicians, 5th ed., ed. Eric Bloom. New York: St. Martin's, 1959, Vol. 1, p. 360.

Hatfield, Edwin F. *The Poets of the Church: A Series of Biographical Sketches of Hymn-Writers with Notes on Their Hymns*. Boston: Milford House, 1972, pp. 682-83.

Studwell, William E. *Christmas Carols: A Reference Guide*. New York: Garland, 1985.

PROPAGATORS OF THE CHRISTMAS CAROL: THE PIONEER HISTORIANS

Edmondstoune Duncan

William E. Studwell
Dorothy Jones

Prior to Edmondstoune Duncan, there had been a fair amount of material published on the history of the carol. For instance, William Sandys's two Christmas classics, *Christmas Carols, Ancient and Modern* (1833) and *Christmastide: Its History, Festivities, and Carols* (1852) contain valuable historical data. So do William Fyfe's useful volume, *Christmas, Its Customs and Carols* (1860), and Bramley and Stainer's two editions of *Christmas Carols, New and Old* (1871, and around 1878).

But Duncan (1866-1920) was the first person to assemble a comprehensive, sizable, and important history of the Christmas carol in the English language. His *The Story of the Carol* (London: Walter Scott Publishing Company, 1911), although flawed, is a definite landmark.

Ironically, though his carol history was one of his more significant accomplishments in the long run, it probably was not looked upon as anything particularly special in his lifetime. He was the author of a number of other works, and also was an organist, pianist, and composer of consequence. Born in Sale, Chesire, William Edmondstoune Duncan demonstrated musical ability early and at 16 became an associate of the Royal College of Organists. The next year he received a scholarship for composition at the just founded Royal College of Music. Up to about 1900, most of his nonroutine activity focused on composition. Among his more noted creations were:

- Concert Overture in D Minor (1888)
- Ye Mariners of England (an ode for chorus and orchestra, 1890)

[Haworth co-indexing entry note]: "Edmondstoune Duncan." Studwell, William E., and Dorothy Jones. Co-published simultaneously in *Music Reference Services Quarterly* (The Haworth Press, Inc.) Vol. 6, No. 4, 1998, pp. 45-48; and: *Publishing Glad Tidings: Essays on Christmas Music* (William E. Studwell, and Dorothy E. Jones) The Haworth Press, Inc., 1998, pp. 45-48. Single or multiple copies of this article are available for a fee from The Haworth Document Delivery Service [1-800-342-9678, 9:00 a.m. - 5:00 p.m. (EST). E-mail address: getinfo@haworth.com].

45

- Mass in F Minor (1892)
- Perseus (an opera, 1892)
- Sonnet to the Nightingale (soprano solo and orchestra, 1895)
- Trio in E Minor (piano and strings, 1895)

After 1900, his nonroutine activity emphasized writing. In addition to *The Story of the Carol*, he also authored or edited:

- Carols and Songs of Christmastide (1902)
- Christmas Album (1901)
- Dancing Songs of the World (1915)
- Encyclopedia of Musical Terms (1914)
- A History of Music (1908)
- Lyrics From the Old Song Books (1927)
- Melodies and How to Harmonize Them (1906)
- The Minstrelsy of England (1905)
- Opera Stories of To-day and Yesterday (1923)
- Schubert (1905)
- The Story of Minstrelsy (1907)
- Ultra-Modernism in Music (1917)

More day-to-day work included a professorship at Oldham College of Music and music criticism for a London daily newspaper. None of his achievements made him especially famous. His compositions, even his opera, are obscure today. Of his books, the biography of Schubert, in the "Master Musicians" series, had several editions and is one of the better treatments of the great composer. Also, *The Story of Minstrelsy* and *The Story of the Carol* are both key works in their respective areas. (Duncan's two carol collections, *Carols and Songs of Christmastide* and *Christmas Album*, were minor and nothing out of the ordinary.)

A fair proportion of his legacy, therefore, was his 1911 carol history. Considering that he was the pioneer, that relatively little had been written before him, his effort was impressive both quantitatively and qualitatively. Duncan's treatise contained xi, 253 pages, many music examples, a biographical appendix, a glossary, a chronological table, an excellent bibliography, and an index. There is much valuable information in the volume, but it has three substantial flaws. It is not well organized, it has some misinformation and questionable points of focus, and it largely ignores the carols of the 19th century, a most important era.

The dubious organization is unfortunate but can be overcome. The misinformation is as a whole understandable in the light of the state of the art at the time. Less comprehensible are some of his choices for emphasis, for instance spending almost a whole page describing and listing the songs published by Irish Bishop Luke Wadding in the late 17th century. Of the 15 songs listed, none is clearly identifiable as an extant carol and only one title even remotely sounds like a carol. (However, one minor carol, "Irish Carol," or "Christmas Day Is Come," was derived from Wadding.) In contrast, soon after that page there is a listing of ten French carols published in about the same period. This list takes up about one quarter of a page. Six of those ten songs cited are identifiable as currently extant and even active carols. In other words, Duncan sometimes pays more attention to the esoteric than is justified.

Even less excusable is Duncan's almost total bypassing of the 19th century, one of the most crucial periods for the carol in England, the United States, and elsewhere. The only 19th-century carol mentioned is "Good King Wenceslas," and probably this inclusion was made because the tune was from the 13th century. By 1911, such 19th-century carols as "Hark! The Herald Angels Sing," "O Holy Night," "Silent Night," "Angels from the Realms of Glory," "What Child Is This?," "Joy to the World," "It Came Upon the Midnight Clear," and "O Little Town of Bethlehem" were all reasonably well known. Yet none of these famous songs, which were either English or had reached England by the first decade of the 20th century, were even mentioned. Although it is always difficult to know how to treat more recent works in any history of music, some effort should be made to be reasonably up to date and current. Basically, Duncan's coverage of carols stops around the end of the 18th century although his bibliography goes up to 1907.

In spite of Edmondstoune Duncan's obsession with older carols, *The Story of the Carol* is a major milestone in the propagation of the Christmas carol. For the first time some one comprehensively and extensively gathered scattered material on the carol's past, and, furthermore, did it reasonably well. When combined with the carol information in John Julia's *A Dictionary of Hymnology*, which first appeared about two decades before, in 1892, a coherent and substantial body of carol history was made available to the general public. Later works, such as *Publications of the Carol Society* (1924-47), *The Oxford Book of Carols* (1928), three carol publications by Richard R. Terry in the early 1930s, and Erik Routley's *The English Carol* (1958), were to be decidedly better and more valuable than Duncan's volume, but *The Story of the Carol* helped pave the way for these carol classics and others. These subsequent publications all owe some debt to Duncan as their harbinger in carol historiography.

BIBLIOGRAPHY

Brown, James Duff and Stephen S. Stratton. *British Musical Biography: A Dictionary of Musical Artists, Authors, and Composers Born in Britain and Its Colonies*. Birmingham: S.S. Stratton. 1897, p. 131.

Duncan, Edmondstoune. *The Story of the Carol*. London: Walter Scott Publishing Co., 1911.

Grove's Dictionary of Music and Musicians, fifth ed., ed. Eric Blom. New York: St. Martin's, 1959, Vol. 2, pp. 803-804.

Charles L. Hutchins

William E. Studwell
Dorothy Jones

At first glance, Charles Lewis Hutchins does not seem to be a carol historian. He readily gives the impression of being a carol compiler and editor of some note, but his role as a historian is far from obvious. Yet when one reviews his most important contribution to the propagation of the Christmas carol, Hutchins's dual role as collector and historian becomes quite evident.

Hutchins (1838-1920) is not very well known or well documented. He was an Episcopal minister and a musician with master of arts and doctor of divinity degrees. By 1874, he was living in the Boston area and stayed there until his death. He began publishing around 1865 and produced, among others, the following volumes:

Annotations of the Hymnal: Consisting of Notes, Biographical Sketches of Authors, Originals and References (1872)

Adjunct publication to the 1872 hymnal of the Protestant Episcopal Church in the U.S.A. Hutchins's propensity towards being a historian was suggested by this early publication.

The Autobiography of Levi Hutchins, with Preface, Notes, and Addenda, by his Youngest Son (1865)

This autobiography edited by Hutchins was the first hint in print of his future historian activities.

[Haworth co-indexing entry note]: "Charles L. Hutchins." Studwell, William E., and Dorothy Jones. Co-published simultaneously in *Music Reference Services Quarterly* (The Haworth Press, Inc.) Vol. 6, No. 4, 1998, pp. 49-52; and: *Publishing Glad Tidings: Essays on Christmas Music* (William E. Studwell, and Dorothy E. Jones) The Haworth Press, Inc., 1998, pp. 49-52. Single or multiple copies of this article are available for a fee from The Haworth Document Delivery Service [1-800-342-9678, 9:00 a.m. - 5:00 p.m. (EST). E-mail address: getinfo@haworth.com].

The Canticles, with the Te Deum, Office of Holy Communion, and Other Services of the Church (1872)

Editing this work required some historical research.

The Chant and Service Book, Containing the Choral Service for Morning and Evening Prayer (1894)

Again, historical digging had to be part of this.

A Church Hymnal (1870)

Unofficial predecessor to the next publication.

The Church Hymnal (1872)

Official hymnal of the Protestant Episcopal Church in the U.S.A., authorized by a general convention in 1871. It had numerous editions (at least 68) and variants. It was revised and enlarged in 1893.

The Church Psalter (1897)

The official Episcopal psalter, which had multiple editions.

The Sunday School Hymnal (1871)

Another multi-edition work.

From these publications it is apparent that the Rev. Hutchins was both talented and ambitious. At the surprisingly young age of 34 he was the editor of the hymnal for a major denomination, and his work with church-related publishing continued throughout his lifetime. For almost half a century he was the editor of *The Parish Choir*, a serial issued from 1874 to about 1919.

Over the years *The Parish Choir* often included texts of Christmas carols. In 1916, Hutchins gathered the songs published in this serial plus a large number of other compositions, and produced a very significant carol collection. Entitled *Carols Old and Carols New: For Use at Christmas and Other Seasons of the Christian Year*, it was issued by the Parish Choir, Boston. In line with Hutchins's long-demonstrated streak of ambition, the hardbound volume was enormous. It was XVII, 659 pages in size, and it contained the astronomical number of 751 carols.

Both the physical size and the number of carols are unmatched, as far as is known, by any single-volume, English-language carol collection either before or after. About 63% of the songs were for Christmas, about 27%

were for Easter, and about 10% were for Ascension/Whitsuntide, Harvest-time, Children's Day, and Flower services. The almost 500 carols for the Christmas season were international in scope, and included both world-wide favorites and uncommon or unique compositions.

Included in the compilation was a printing of "Angels We Have Heard on High," the best known English translation of the anonymous/folk 18th-century French carol "Les anges dans nos compagnes." The original translation was published in 1862, but varied considerably from the pres-ent version. The 1916 printing may well have been the first appearance of the familiar English rendition.

Also included in the collection was a notable body of material which made Hutchins one of the more important pioneering carol historians as well as an extraordinary carol compiler. In addition to a preface, Hutch-ins's huge volume contained an author, translator, and text source index, a composer and music source index, a first-line index, a valuable four-page bibliography which included a number of older or unusual items, and a moderate amount of data on the authorship of the carols.

To us today this may not seem to be anything exceptional, yet at the time it was unique. Some prior collections had included indexes or small amounts of historical data, for example, Bramley and Stainer's 1871 and circa 1878 editions of *Christmas Carols, New and Old*. (The similarity between this title and Hutchins's *Carols Old and Carols New* suggests the possible influence of Bramley and Stainer on Hutchins.) But no carol collection before the superlative *Oxford Book of Carols* (1928) even ap-proached the amount of historical information which could be found in Hutchins's 1916 classic.

Yet Hutchins's *Carols Old and Carols New* is little known and copies of it in the late 20th century are relatively rare. Only 1,000 were printed, a very modest number considering the mass marketing of other collections. The issuance of the volume when Hutchins was 78, past the age of youth-ful vigor, probably inhibited subsequent editions. His death four years after the collection's publication completely shut off any possibility of reprinting. The small number of copies limited its fame, and twelve years later *The Oxford Book of Carols*, the world's greatest carol compilation, completely overwhelmed any opportunities for more renown.

However, Charles Lewis Hutchins was the first carol editor to incorpo-rate a substantial amount of historical material in a volume of Christmas carols. Although not nearly as scholarly or valuable as *The Oxford Book*, it did get to the historical starting line over a decade before *Oxford*.

BIBLIOGRAPHY

Carols Old and Carols New: For Use at Christmas and Other Seasons of the Christian Year. Collected from many sources and arranged by the Rev. Charles L. Hutchins. Boston: The Parish Choir, 1916.

Studwell, William E., and Dorothy Jones. "Obscure Carol Classics I: Charles Hutchins' Carols Old and Carols New," *The Choral Journal*, Vol. 29, No. 1 (August 1988). pp. 11-14.

Edward Bliss Reed

William E. Studwell
Dorothy Jones

If the Carol Society were still in existence, the authors of this essay would be enthusiastic members of the organization. Unfortunately, the society ceased to exist around 1947, when the last of its 19 volumes of carols was published. When Edward Bliss Reed (1872-1940), secretary of the society and the main force in its founding and continuance, died, the heart of the group apparently went with him. Although three of the Carol Society volumes were published after he was gone, they obviously were projects already in motion by 1940.

The Carol Society was founded in New Haven, Conn., in 1923 with one clear purpose–to "recover, publish, or circulate old Christmas carols and to encourage carol singing." To that end the society issued a series of English-language carol collections published annually from 1924 to 1939, plus post-Reed volumes in 1941, 1942, and 1947. Each volume was around 36 pages and contained eight carols with accompanying historical notes. Reed was the translator and historian for the first 16 volumes, and David Stanley Smith provided competent and usable musical arrangements. After Reed's death, Alfred Raymond Bellinger did the translations and notes for the final three volumes, and Luther M. Noss (Vols. 17 and 18) and Marshall Bartholomew (Vol. 19) did the music arrangements. The publisher role was in like manner split into two segments, with Stainer & Bell, London, printing the first 16 volumes, and Galaxy Music Corporation, New York, the last three.

Altogether, the *Publications of the Carol Society* printed 152 folk carols from a variety of cultures. Generally the carols are uncommon or not well

[Haworth co-indexing entry note]: "Edward Bliss Reed." Studwell, William E., and Dorothy Jones. Co-published simultaneously in *Music Reference Services Quarterly* (The Haworth Press, Inc.) Vol. 6, No. 4, 1998, pp. 53-56; and: *Publishing Glad Tidings: Essays on Christmas Music* (William E. Studwell, and Dorothy E. Jones) The Haworth Press, Inc., 1998, pp. 53-56. Single or multiple copies of this article are available for a fee from The Haworth Document Delivery Service [1-800-342-9678, 9:00 a.m. - 5:00 p.m. (EST). E-mail address: getinfo@haworth.com].

known and a number of them are found in no other publications. But it is not just for the preservation of old carols that the *Publications of the Carol Society* should be appreciated. The very high quality of the 19 issues, that is, excellent historical scholarship and artistically tasteful translations and arrangements, makes the Carol Society an outstanding though shortlived cultural force.

The individual titles in the series were:

1. Eight Traditional French Noëls
2. Eight Traditional Christmas Carols
3. Old French and Franconian Carols
4. Old French and German Carols
5. Old Christmas Carols
6. Traditional Christmas Carols
7. Old French and Polish Carols
8. Old French and Czechoslovakian Christmas Carols
9. Traditional Basque and Flemish Christmas Carols
10. Russian, Basque, and Flemish Carols
11. Swiss, English, and Swedish Carols
12. Provençal and Russian Carols
13. Eight Old Christmas Carols
14. Old Carols for Christmas
15. Flemish and Other Christmas Carols
16. Provençal and Other Christmas Carols
17. Eight Swiss and French Carols
18. Eight French and Flemish Carols
19. Eight Burgundian Carols

Due to the limited distribution of the series as well as its duration of about two decades, the *Publications of the Carol Society* and its guiding light Reed are about as obscure as the majority of the carols printed. Reed, long associated with Yale University, is not very well known for his other achievements either. Valedictorian of the 1894 class at Yale and editor of the class book, Reed showed academic, especially literary, promise early. Most of his publications related to literature, but his interest and capabilities in cultural history also were evident. Among the books he wrote or edited were:

Christmas Carols Printed in the Sixteenth Century (1932)

Reed edited this small scholarly volume of minor importance. Included were reproductions of carols printed by Englishman Richard Kele, who died in 1552.

The Commonwealth Fund Fellows and Their Impression of America (1932)

On U.S. history and civilization. Another minor publication edited by Reed.

English Lyrical Poetry from Its Origins to the Present Time (1912)

Significant historical survey of English poetry.

Lyra Levis (1922)

Reed's own poetry.

Lyra Yalensis (1913)

Reed's poems about Yale.

Sea Moods and Other Poems (1917)

More of Reed's poetry.

Seven Hundred French Terms for American Field Artillerymen (1917)

For use in World War I.

Songs from the British Drama (1925)

A collection of English songs edited by Reed.

Reed also edited poetry collections of Thomas Fairfax, Alexander Pope, and William Shakespeare, plus a selection of prose works by Joseph Addison. His substantial experience with literary and historical topics, and his apparent love of carols, made him an ideal leader for the Carol Society.

Since in reality the Carol Society and Edward Bliss Reed cannot be effectively separated, the story of the valuable contributions of the society equates to homage for this key but underappreciated figure in the history of carols. For his role in the society and for his exceptional historical scholarship, he is one of the more important propagators of the Christmas carol. His historical research compared favorably with that of Percy Dearmer in the superlative classic *The Oxford Book of Carols* (1928). But the chap from the American colonies preceded his noted English counterparts by about four years. At least in the matter of chronological sequence, Reed actually beat the English at one of the tasks they do so very well–carol printing and historiography in extraordinary style.

BIBLIOGRAPHY

Publications of the Carol Society. London: Stainer & Bell, etc., 1924-47 (19 vols.).

Studwell, William E., and Dorothy Jones, "Obscure Carol Classics III: Publications of the Carol Society." *The Choral Journal* 29, No. 3 (Oct. 1988). pp. 5-8.

PROPAGATORS
OF THE CHRISTMAS CAROL:
THE "OXFORD BOOK" TRIO

Percy Dearmer

Dorothy Jones
William E. Studwell

Percy Dearmer might have been every contemporary church musician's ideal clerical colleague. One of the preeminent concerns of Dearmer's life and career was that there be a right relationship between art and religion. His interest in the arts embraced the visual arts and architecture, the beauty of the spoken word, and the real and lasting influence of music on the spirit of the worshiper. He understood the importance and mission of music in the church. For him, music in the church was not just an ornament or a mood maker. It was an essential act of worship, integral to the service and to one's need to offer the best he has and is.

Born in 1867, the son of an artist, Dearmer read history at Christ Church, Oxford, was ordained a deacon in 1891 and a priest in 1892. After several curacies, he became vicar of St. Mary's, Primrose Hill, in 1901, and remained there for 14 years. His efforts to vitalize liturgy and ceremony were both effective and productive of publications such as the 1904 *Servers Handbook*, *The Ornaments of the Ministers* in 1908, and the 1906 *English Hymnal*, which he helped edit. A prolific author and editor, many publications of this and later periods of his life were reissued in several editions. St. Mary's became a gathering place for artists and musicians.

A second dominant interest for Dearmer, next to art in religion, was the social mission of the church. He was secretary to the London Christian Social Union, chaplain to the British Red Cross in Serbia, and was personally involved in the YMCA Mission of Help in India and in lectures in France, India, Japan, and the U.S.

Percy Dearmer lost both his wife and the younger of two sons during

[Haworth co-indexing entry note]: "Percy Dearmer." Jones, Dorothy, and William E. Studwell. Co-published simultaneously in *Music Reference Services Quarterly* (The Haworth Press, Inc.) Vol. 6, No. 4, 1998, pp. 59-61; and: *Publishing Glad Tidings: Essays on Christmas Music* (William E. Studwell, and Dorothy E. Jones) The Haworth Press, Inc., 1998, pp. 59-61. Single or multiple copies of this article are available for a fee from The Haworth Document Delivery Service [1-800-342-9678, 9:00 a.m. - 5:00 p.m. (EST). E-mail address: getinfo@haworth.com].

World War I, when he was a chaplain in Serbia. His wife, Jessie Mabel, a writer, succumbed to enteric fever in Serbia, and his son died of wounds received at Gallipoli. Dearmer married his second wife, Nancy Knowles, in 1916. They had two daughters and one son.

After the war, he was appointed the first professor of ecclesiastical art at King's College, London, became active in the League of Arts, was involved with the founding of Guildhouse, and did a good deal of writing. In 1931, he became a canon of Westminster, where he continued in active ministry emphasizing the arts and social concerns until his death in 1936.

Dearmer's list of publications reveals a stunning breadth of knowledge, interests, and talent. He wrote on history, social issues, liturgy, and art. He wrote *The Dragon of Wessex: a Novel* in 1911, *A First Russian Reader* in 1915, and *The Christmas Party, a Play* in 1926. Tucked in among well over 50 publications are his contributions to hymnology, church music, and more specifically, to the Christmas carol repertoire. His *Songs of Praise*, 1925 and later editions, was a major contribution to congregational singing. He produced the *English Carol Book* in 1913, and the *English Carol Book* Second Series in 1919. Finally, he was an editor of that classic foundation of every choir director's music library, *The Oxford Book of Carols* (1928).

The *Dictionary of National Biography* credits Dearmer with being "largely responsible" for editing the *Oxford Book of Carols*, even though his coeditors were prominent composers Ralph Vaughan Williams and Martin Shaw. Dearmer was a man of mission, both in his Christian social concerns and his conviction of the power of art and music to inspire and express faith. It was he who persuaded Ralph Vaughan Williams to work on *The English Hymnal* of 1906. Vaughan Williams writes of his first meeting with Dearmer: "It must have been in 1904 that I was sitting in my study in Barton Street, Westminster, when a cab drove up to the door and Mr. Dearmer was announced. I just knew his name vaguely as a parson who invited tramps to sleep in his drawing room; but he had not come to me about tramps. He went straight to the point and asked me to edit the music of a hymnbook. I protested that I knew very little about hymns but he explained to me that Cecil Sharp had suggested my name, and I found out afterwards that Canon Scott Holland had also suggested me as a possible editor, and the final clench was given when I understood that if I did not do the job it would be offered to a well-known church musician with whose musical ideas I was much out of sympathy" (Ursula Vaughan Williams, pp. 70-71).

This was the first collaboration of Dearmer and Williams, preceding *Songs of Praise* and *The Oxford Book of Carols*. Dearmer was more scholar, translator, and historian, and we look for his contribution, not in the composition or arrangement of tunes, but in preface, translations, and word editing.

Percy Dearmer said, in his preface to the eleventh edition of *The Parson's Handbook*, that "a true philosophy of values shows us that beauty is necessary to a right life. . . ." Percy Dearmer's life was lived enjoying beauty, creating beauty, and, most of all, propagating the idea of beauty as a necessary and fitting offering to his Creator.

BIBLIOGRAPHY

Dearmer, Percy. *The Parson's Handbook*, 11th edition. London, 1928.
Dictionary of National Biography 1931-1940, ed. L.G. Wickham Legg. London: Oxford University Press, 1949, pp. 216-17.
Scholes, Percy A. *Oxford Companion to Music*, 10th edition. revised, reset, and edited by John Owen Ward. London: Oxford University Press, 1974. p. 281.
Vaughan Williams, Ursula, *R.V.W.: A Biography of Ralph Vaughan Williams*. London: Oxford University Press, 1964.
Who Was Who, Vol. III, 1929-1940. London: Adam and Charles Black, 1947, p. 345.

Ralph Vaughan Williams

Dorothy Jones
William E. Studwell

Ralph Vaughan Williams, born October 12, 1872, is known as one of England's most influential nationalistic composers, discovering and collecting music of the English countryside and using tunes of the people as the core or inspiration for much of his creative work. He was an Englishman's Englishman. His family tree is well sprinkled with "Sirs" and he numbers Josiah Wedgewood and Charles Darwin among his forebears. His education was impeccable (Charterhouse, Trinity College, Cambridge, Royal College of Music). The professions most often embraced by members of his family were in law or the church. Vaughan Williams was a thinker of independence and integrity, interested in traditions and folk history, but impatient of narrowness and intolerance. He refused knighthood and declined to succeed Elgar as Master of the King's Music. Publicly protesting against the BBC's banning of a composer's music because of that composer's political views, Vaughan Williams withdrew a song the BBC had commissioned and returned the fee they had paid him (Ursula Vaughan Williams, p. 239).

Ralph Vaughan Williams was born into a country parsonage. At the death of his father when Ralph was two years old, his mother moved, with her three children, back to her family home at Leith Hill Place in Surrey. His Aunt Sophy gave him his first music lessons and there was much pleasurable, domestic music making. As a youth, he loved Christmas carols, and these were an integral part of family musicales and church singing. Ralph played piano, organ, violin, and viola–but was never a brilliant performer. He studied many years at the Royal College of Music

---

[Haworth co-indexing entry note]: "Ralph Vaughan Williams." Jones, Dorothy, and William E. Studwell. Co-published simultaneously in *Music Reference Services Quarterly* (The Haworth Press, Inc.) Vol. 6, No. 4, 1998, pp. 63-65; and: *Publishing Glad Tidings: Essays on Christmas Music* (William E. Studwell, and Dorothy E. Jones) The Haworth Press, Inc., 1998, pp. 63-65. Single or multiple copies of this article are available for a fee from The Haworth Document Delivery Service [1-800-342-9678, 9:00 a.m. - 5:00 p.m. (EST). E-mail address: getinfo@haworth.com].

and at Trinity College, Cambridge. "Few composers have had so prolonged a period of formal education; and probably none of real distinction has been regarded quite so gloomily by his teachers" (Ottaway, p. 7). He was a person who needed lots of time–time to develop, to explore, to learn. He was aware of this need. Vaughan Williams was not a child prodigy, nor did he have that sparkling, obvious talent which lends itself to quick success as an adult. Ottaway, in his short biography, states that "If Vaughan Williams had died at the same age as Purcell, Mozart, or Schubert, he would be merely a name in the musical histories, a minor figure among the English composers at the turn of the century. At 40 he had only recently found his direction" (Ottaway, p. 3). It was his love of music and his persistent and determined spirit that finally forced the emergence of a great, latent talent.

Vaughan Williams produced a large body of compositions, including symphonies, songs, ballets, operas, chamber music, and choral music. While he certainly benefited from studies abroad, and was eclectic in his tastes and interests, he became convinced that English music could and should be revitalized–and revitalized from within. In 1903 he turned to the folk songs of England and found his niche. He became one of the great folk song collectors. His love of the English folk song is apparent in his works, both as a subtle influence and as a direct source.

One of Vaughan Williams's major contributions to music was his coeditorship, along with Percy Dearmer and Martin Shaw, of *The Oxford Book of Carols*. Vaughan Williams first worked with Percy Dearmer on *The English Hymnal* of 1906. This was a much longer, more involved, more expensive, and more creative project than either man had expected. It is our good fortune that they were willing to tackle other somewhat similar projects, one of which was *The Oxford Book of Carols*. In Vaughan Williams's contribution to this valuable collection, one can see the commingling of the family musicales of his childhood, his conviction that the music of ordinary people is important, and his years of scholarship. *The Oxford Book of Carols* has gone through several editions and has been reprinted dozens of times. While it has never been considered the primary publication of its editors, and has in fact often been omitted from their lists of publications, it has probably touched more individuals, choirs, and congregations than any other single work produced by any of the three editors.

BIBLIOGRAPHY

Day, James. *Vaughan Williams*. London: J.M. Dent and Sons Ltd., 1961.
Dictionary of National Biography 1951-1960, ed. E.T. Williams and Helen M. Palmer. London: Oxford University Press, 1971, pp. 1,006-1,009.
Ottaway, Hugh. *Vaughan Williams*. London: Novello and Company Ltd., 1966.

The Oxford Book of Carols, ed. Percy Dearmer, R. Vaughan Williams, and Martin Shaw. London: Oxford University Press, 1928.

Vaughan Williams, Ursula, *R.V.W.: A Biography of Ralph Vaughan Williams.* London: Oxford University Press, 1964.

Who Was Who 1951-1960. London: Adam and Charles Black, 1961, p. 1,115.

Martin Shaw

Dorothy Jones
William E. Studwell

Martin Shaw, one of the distinguished triumvirate who gave us *The Oxford Book of Carols*, was born in London on March 9, 1875, and died in Southwold on October 24, 1958, at age 83. He traveled an orthodox educational route to his profession. He was a student at the Royal Academy of Music, along with Ralph Vaughan Williams and Gustav Holst, and studied composition under Sir Charles Stanford. He was an organist and composer who participated purposefully and effectively in the musical life of his time through societies, writing, and conversation with colleagues.

The three editors of *The Oxford Book of Carols*–Percy Dearmer, Ralph Vaughan Williams, and Martin Shaw–each had unique professional objectives which seem to have prompted them to accept the tremendous amount of work which was required to edit both *The Oxford Book of Carols* in 1928 and *Songs of Praise* in 1931. Percy Dearmer was a theologian who cared deeply about the conjunction and blending of religion, beauty, and art. Ralph Vaughan Williams cared deeply about the renewal of English music and found a means of renewal through applying his talent and scholarship to English folk music, carols, and traditional tunes of the church. Martin Shaw had a commitment to church music, to "average" congregations, and to "Englishness."

Martin Shaw was described by Erik Routley as a man "whose special distinction it was to restore to English church music the quality of being English," a man who most profoundly believed in "the virtues of being English" (Routley, p. 1). Shaw's enthusiastic and concentrated efforts toward strengthening awareness and pride in English culture are reflected

[Haworth co-indexing entry note]: "Martin Shaw." Jones, Dorothy, and William E. Studwell. Co-published simultaneously in *Music Reference Services Quarterly* (The Haworth Press, Inc.) Vol. 6, No. 4, 1998, pp. 67-69; and: *Publishing Glad Tidings: Essays on Christmas Music* (William E. Studwell, and Dorothy E. Jones) The Haworth Press, Inc., 1998, pp. 67-69. Single or multiple copies of this article are available for a fee from The Haworth Document Delivery Service [1-800-342-9678, 9:00 a.m. - 5:00 p.m. (EST). E-mail address: getinfo@haworth.com].

in the following observation made by Erik Routley 17 years after Shaw's death: "Name any British composer who is getting published now, be he eminent or as avant-garde as you like; Martin Shaw helped to make the world safe for him" (Routley, p. 10). While Shaw's published works, some 300 in number, include school and secular songs, he had a special commitment to music for the Church of England. Concerning Shaw's contribution to *Songs of Praise* and *The Oxford Book of Carols*, Routley writes: "It is probably safe to say that Martin Shaw never in all his strenuous work for English music did it a greater service than he did in the second of these books. . . . [He] injected something into the English church culture which irreversibly transformed it. This was the celebration of authentic folk song and authentic English music" (Routley, p. 6).

There were several family members who had a very strong influence on Shaw's musical-professional life. One such person was his father, James Shaw, a composer and organist working first in Edinburgh and then in London. Shaw's brother, Geoffrey, was also a well-known musician specializing in music for schools and for training purposes. Martin Shaw's marriage in 1916 to Joan Cobbold, talented daughter of an aristocratic family, marked the beginning of a particularly creative and musically productive period in his life.

Colleagues were also very influential in Shaw's development. Three in particular might be mentioned as people who strengthened Shaw's own impetus to accomplishment in the areas of music for the common man, music which was truly English, and music for renewal in the church. These three are Gordon Craig, Ralph Vaughan Williams, and Percy Dearmer. Gordon Craig was a vastly energetic dramatist and man of the theater who persuaded Shaw to leave his organ post in 1903 and join the world of theater. Shaw traveled with Craig, conducting theater orchestras. From 1906 to 1908 he was musical director for Isadora Duncan, traveling extensively in Europe. Ralph Vaughan Williams was a collaborator and loyal friend who shared, with less intensity, Shaw's zeal for English music. Finally, there was Percy Dearmer, who worked so hard to encourage the artistic aspect of worship and who was instrumental in Shaw's return to organ and church in 1908. Both Dearmer and Shaw were vitally interested in liturgy and intellectual evangelism in the church. They worked on experimental preaching services and on collections of hymns that would be new but liked by the average congregation.

Shaw wanted people in the smallest congregation to have good music, and he wanted good composers to write church music that all people could sing. He himself "was a composer of absolutely faultless integrity, who so limited and restrained his talent as to make it accessible to ordinary choirs of children, schools and parishes, and to ordinary singers in ordinary pews" (Routley, p. 10). *The Oxford Book of Carols*, which bears the mark of his selection and editing talents, is testimony to his passion for fine English music made accessible and singable for ordinary people.

BIBLIOGRAPHY

Routley, Erik. *Martin Shaw: A Centenary Appreciation*. London: E.M. Campbell, 1975.
The New Grove Dictionary of Music, ed. Stanley Sadie. London: Macmillan. 1980, p. 234.
Who Was Who 1951-1960. London: Adam and Charles Black, 1961, p. 990.

OTHER TWENTIETH CENTURY CAROL EXPERTS

George Ratcliffe Woodward, Editor of *The Cowley Carol Books*

Dorothy E. Jones
William E. Studwell

The Rev. George Ratcliffe Woodward (1848-1934) was influential in the late 19th-century movement to renew interest in English church music and restore it to a position of respect by means of historical research, the resurrection of the finest music of the past, and the creation of new music of solid quality. Woodward's interest in church music, and his concern for excellence, embraced a popular form of music–the carol. He was a collector, editor, translator, and author of carols and was a collaborator and good friend of the composer Charles Wood. Wood concentrated primarily on church music and his texts included many hymns and translations by Woodward (Long, pp. 377-78). Woodward, while primarily a scholar and author, also contributed some settings and harmonizations to the collections of hymns and carols that he edited. Erik Routley, in his book, *Twentieth Century Church Music*, gives credit to Woodward for a scholarly approach to a renewed interest in carols: "Another characteristically 20th-century development is the increased, and still increasing, interest in singing carols. As is more fully explained in my book, *The English Carol*, this movement has its roots in the early 19th century; but a scholarly approach to it was introduced by G.R. Woodward in his *Cowley Carol Book* . . . "(Routley, p. 106).

The Cowley Carol Book: for Christmas, Easter and Ascensiontide was published under Woodward's editorship in the autumn of 1901. He produced this little volume in response to a specific request for a small

[Haworth co-indexing entry note]: "George Ratcliffe Woodward, Editor of *The Cowley Carol Books*." Jones, Dorothy E., and William E. Studwell. Co-published simultaneously in *Music Reference Services Quarterly* (The Haworth Press, Inc.) Vol. 6, No. 4, 1998, pp. 73-75; and: *Publishing Glad Tidings: Essays on Christmas Music* (William E. Studwell, and Dorothy E. Jones) The Haworth Press, Inc., 1998, pp. 73-75. Single or multiple copies of this article are available for a fee from The Haworth Document Delivery Service [1-800-342-9678, 9:00 a.m. - 5:00 p.m. (EST). E-mail address: getinfo@haworth.com].

volume of carols for use in the Church of St. John the Evangelist, Cowley *(Cowley Carol Book*, Preface, First Series). It contained 39 carols and it was followed very quickly by a second edition in 1902. The second edition was expanded to include 65 carols, and some of the harmonies of the first edition were altered. In 1919, another set of 37 carols was published as *The Cowley Carol Book: for Christmas, Easter and Ascensiontide*, Second Series, compiled and arranged by George Ratcliffe Woodward and Charles Wood.

During the years between the first and second series of the *Cowley Carol Book*, George Woodward edited *Songs of Syon*. The title page speaks for Woodward's erudite, precise approach to his work and his desire to present period music in as authentic a form as possible. It reads: *Songs of Syon: A Collection of Psalms, Hymns & Spiritual Songs set, for the most part, to their Ancient Proper Tunes.* The title, *Songs of Syon*, is itself an ancient phrase taken from the Bible, Psalm 137, verse 3: "For there they that carried us away captive required of us a song: and they that wasted us required of us mirth, saying, Sing us one of the Songs of Zion" (King James Version). Kenneth R. Long says," . . . it is one of the most erudite and austere Anglo-Catholic collections ever published, a monument of careful scholarship, wide culture, and sensitive imagination. Its editor, the Rev. G.R. Woodward, was a disciple of J.M. Neale and had a similarly medieval cast of mind. His purpose was 'to raise the standard of English taste by rescuing from oblivion some of the finest melodies of the 16th, 17th, and 18th centuries.' To carry these tunes, many of which were in unusual meters, he provided 'a collection of hymns and sacred poems mostly translated from ancient Greek, Latin, and German sources' (50 or so of them from his own pen). Plainsong hymns were printed in square notes on four-lined staves and no accompaniment was provided; older tunes appeared without bar lines, and chorales were given in Bach's most florid harmonizations. *Songs of Syon* was planned only as a supplementary volume to other more general hymnals but it was quickly recognized as an important source book and has been drawn on by most subsequent compilers" (Long, p. 401). Woodward says, in his preface to the fourth edition of *Songs of Syon*," . . . concerning the Style of the Harmonies. It is frankly avowed that these are mostly old-fashioned. With a bold disregard for later conventionalities, the harmonies of each earlier age have been purposely retained. That which may sound as a 'false relation' to modern ears was not disagreeable to the taste of our musical forefathers, who rejoiced in the *Tierce de Picardie*, who delighted in 'open fifths,' and were not averse from 'consecutive octaves' and 'parallel quints,' when these occurred between the end of one phrase and the beginning of another. The Editor believes that there is room for a book containing specimens of the work, both melodic and harmonic, of bygone ages" (Woodward, Preface, p. iv). Modes are identified and sources of tunes and words are carefully cited over the head of each carol or hymn.

Interestingly, the *Cowley Carol Books* do not have any Advent carols, while *Songs of Syon*, a general hymnbook, has many Advent carols and one to which Woodward gave a special heading of "Christmas-Even." The latter begins, "Toll! toll! because there ends tonight an empire old and vast" (Woodward, p. 18). It is a special Christmas Eve song!

While Charles Wood seems to have become much better known than George Woodward, it is to Woodward that we owe our thanks for these wonderful collections of carols and hymns. There has been very little written about the Rev. Woodward's personal life. He is not included in major English biographical reference books. He had a great love for the church and for music and a proclivity for thoroughness and accuracy in scholarship. He joyously and gratefully gave credit to all who assisted him in his work. These traits are made evident in prefaces to his collections or in brief references contained in books on the history of church music. They are the traits of a man of rectitude with a sense of purpose. The knowledge that he had contributed significantly to the cause he embraced was more important than great personal recognition. He was a gracious editor whose scholarly commitment and pursuits made a difference.

The preface to *Songs of Syon* ends with these words: "Lastly, the Editor asks the singers and readers of his *Songs of Syon*, of their charity, to remember him sometimes in their prayers during his lifetime, and to bid for the repose of his soul after death" (Woodward, Preface, p. iv).

BIBLIOGRAPHY

The Cowley Carol Book: for Christmas, Easter and Ascensiontide, First Series. Compiled and arranged by George Ratcliffe Woodward. Oxford: A.R. Mowbray and Co. Ltd., 1933.

The Cowley Carol Book: for Christmas, Easter and Ascensiontide, Second Series. Compiled and arranged by George Ratcliffe Woodward and Charles Wood. Oxford: A.R. Mowbray and Co. Ltd., 1931.

Long, Kenneth R., *The Music of the English Church.* London: Hodder and Stoughton, 1971.

Routley, Erik, *Twentieth Century Church Music.* New York: Oxford University Press, 1964.

Woodward, Rev. G.R., ed., *Songs of Syon.* 4th ed., revised and enlarged. London: Schott and Co., 1923.

Richard Runciman Terry

Dorothy Jones
William E. Studwell

Sir Richard Runciman Terry was born in Ellington, Northumberland in 1865 and died in London in 1938. His father was a schoolmaster. His mother came from a seafaring family, and young Richard listened to, and loved, the tales and songs of the sea that he heard from visiting relatives. Both of his parents were amateur musicians and held weekly musical gatherings in their home, during which Richard's bedroom door was left open so that he could listen and enjoy. His mother died when he was eight years old. His upbringing, with his two brothers and two sisters, was then shared by various relatives. Terry's youthful enthusiasms seem to have been almost equally divided between athletics and music, and his commitment to music as a profession did not come until his mid-20s.

Richard Terry was respected and well recognized as a talented and influential musician in his own lifetime. His was a personality which could persuade others, and he was able to draw from his choirs the best they had to give. He seems to have been a man of many contradictions. He was an organist who disliked the organ, but whose talent for fine accompaniment, particularly of Tudor music and plainsong, was widely recognized and whose style was emulated. He was a scholar, but his goals were those of a practical musician. His research was instrumental in reviving music of the Latin ritual by early English composers such as Byrd and Tallis. However, his purpose in translating old manuscripts and part books into usable editions was not to produce scholarly editions but to enlarge the repertoire of his choirs and share the music he loved with the worshipers in his cathedral. His personal life also reflected paradoxical characteristics.

[Haworth co-indexing entry note]: "Richard Runciman Terry." Jones, Dorothy, and William E. Studwell. Co-published simultaneously in *Music Reference Services Quarterly* (The Haworth Press, Inc.) Vol. 6, No. 4, 1998, pp. 77-80; and: *Publishing Glad Tidings: Essays on Christmas Music* (William E. Studwell, and Dorothy E. Jones) The Haworth Press, Inc., 1998, pp. 77-80. Single or multiple copies of this article are available for a fee from The Haworth Document Delivery Service [1-800-342-9678, 9:00 a.m. - 5:00 p.m. (EST). E-mail address: getinfo@haworth.com].

In 1890, after having spent a year at Oxford and two years at King's College, Cambridge, on a choral scholarship, Terry abandoned his studies and took a position as organist and choirmaster at Elstow School near Bedford. The boys and staff liked him very much and it became apparent that he had an unusual talent for choir training and for communicating his musical ideas so that amateur singers could produce inspiring performances. Two years later he went to the West Indies as organist at St. John's Cathedral, Antigua. He reveled in the joys of a new and exotic place with lots of social activity and island sports. While in Antigua, he also delved deeply into the library of a friend who was an Irish Catholic priest. He was profoundly influenced and gradually moved towards the conversion that was so central to the rest of his life and career. He returned to England in 1893. In 1896, he was received into the Church of Rome and began a career which led to international fame. As director of music at the Benedictine School of Downside, he developed a wonderful choir and taught them the music of the 16th-century composers which he unearthed at various libraries and then published. He spent much of the rest of his life finding, editing, and performing little-known music of the Tudor polyphonic school. In 1901, he was appointed organist and director of music in the newly built Westminster Cathedral. The beauty of the music at the cathedral became a focus of attention and his revival of early English liturgical music became a powerful influence on young composers. He was a generous man, well loved by his choirmen, choristers, and young composers for his support of and appreciation for talent, both professional and amateur. Terry received an honorary doctor of music degree from Durham University in 1911 and a knighthood in 1922.

Terry left Westminster Cathedral in 1924. In an article in the *Morning Post* of April 9, 1924, he wrote: "Whereas the revival of our Tudor composers was sneered at as a pursuit for cranks 23 years ago, these same composers are now recognized among the glories of Britain. Whatever may be their fate at Westminster is not now a matter of such consequence as it formerly was. The Tudor movement has extended throughout the country, far outside the four walls of the cathedral. It will now move on of its own momentum" (Andrews, p. 138).

Terry also had another musical mission–the improvement of English Catholic hymnology and the revival of carol singing. Old hymns and carols had been lost or had moved over into the Anglican Church so long ago that there was little or no collective memory of the Catholic hymns and carols of the past. He contributed much to the revival of hymns, carols, and liturgical music. R.R. Terry published *Gilbert and Sandys' Christmas Carols* (London: Burns, Oates and Washbourne) and also *A*

Medieval Carol Book (London: Burns, Oates and Washbourne, 1932). The latter was a collection of melodies, chiefly from manuscripts which he found in the Bodleian Library and in the library of Trinity College, Cambridge. In 1933, *Two Hundred Folk Carols* was published, again by Burns, Oates and Washbourne. This was a huge compilation of European carols garnered by Terry from many sources. It included sacred and secular carols, and "the pure and beautiful modal accompaniments at which he was unsurpassed" (Andrews, p. 148). It contained "sixty-eight English carols, eighteen French carols, ten Besançon carols, eleven Bernaise and Burgundian carols, thirteen Provençal carols, eighteen Basque carols, nineteen Dutch and Flemish carols, ten Italian carols, twenty-one German, Alsatian, and Polish carols, twelve European medieval carols, and two good indexes" (Studwell, p 19). In his preface (p. vii), Terry writes: "This collection has been primarily compiled for the use of choirs, but it cannot be too strongly emphasized that all the carols–save the definitely polyphonic ones (e.g., those of Praetorius)–can be effectively sung as solos, or by voices in unison, with or without accompaniment. The bulk of them are folk melodies, and should be treated as such. Even the carols of Praetorius are simple harmonizations of popular melodies."

The quality of Terry's carol collections is consistently fine, whether one is examining the 49-page *Gilbert and Sandys' Christmas Carols with Six Collateral Tunes* or the massive 395-page *Two Hundred Folk Carols*. These carol books were and are a boon to scholars, but Terry intended that they be used by choirs, congregations, and carolers. Some carols are presented in four-part harmony, but many are presented in unison to be sung with or without his fine accompaniments.

Richard Terry was a significant contributor to the world of music, dedicating himself to the task of introducing something good and beautiful into the lives of his contemporaries and to reviving interest in long-neglected composers and folk music. It was written of Terry that "when he died on Easter Sunday of 1938, Death, freeing him from the tangle of busy affairs in which life had enmeshed him, found him at peace and in great-hearted humility" (Andrews, p. 178).

BIBLIOGRAPHY

Andrews, Hilda. *Westminster Retrospect: A Memoir of Sir Richard Terry*. London: Oxford University Press, 1948.

Legg, L.G., ed. *Dictionary of National Biography, 1931-1940*. London: Oxford University Press, 1949, pp. 853-54.

Long, Kenneth R. *The Music of the English Church*. London: Hodder and Stoughton, c. 1971.

Routley, Erik. *Twentieth Century Church Music*. New York: Oxford University Press, 1964.

Sadie, Stanley, ed. *The New Grove Dictionary of Music and Musicians*, Vol. 18. London: MacMillan, 1980, pp. 698-99.

Studwell, William E., and Dorothy Jones. "Obscure Carol Classics II: Richard Terry's *Two Hundred Folk Carols*," *Choral Journal*, Vol. 29, No. 2 (Sept. 1988), pp. 19-22.

Terry, Richard Runciman, ed. *Two Hundred Folk Carols*. London: Burns, Oates and Washbourne, c. 1933.

Who Was Who, 1929-1940. London: Adam and Charles Black, 1947, pp. 1334-35.

John Jacob Niles

Dorothy Jones
William E. Studwell

If John Jacob Niles had done no more than written "I Wonder as I Wander," he would have given millions a little gift of peace, faith, and delight. But he collected thousands of folk songs, arranged many of them, manufactured dulcimers and lutes on which to perform them, and traveled over Europe and America giving concerts and lectures. Helen Shea Johnson calls Niles the "great-grandfather of ballad-makers, the man who set the pattern and beat the path for nearly every singer of folk songs in the past 70 years" (Johnson, p. 13).

Niles–student, scholar, composer, performer, and recording artist–packed concert halls, published many collections of folk songs, and became an authority who influenced decades of folk and country music artists. He himself remained always a man of the Kentucky Mountains, living with his wife and sons at Boot Hill Farm near Lexington, Kentucky, in a house he helped craft with care and imagination, and with his own hands. He "carved the prayer of St. Francis into one side of his hand-pegged study door: 'Lord, make me an instrument of Thy peace . . . ,' and on the other side, a bluebird flying across a field of flowers surmounted in flowing script: 'For Rena at Christmastime, 1955' " (Johnson, p. 13). On the entrance door of his home were carved tobacco leaves which framed the words: "This house (which is the home of John Jacob Niles, Rena L. Niles, John Edward Niles, and Thomas Michael Tolliver Niles) is dedicated to the balladry of the Anglo-Saxon people, which in elder times has celebrated the prowess and cheered the halls of our gallant ancestors, and having also cheered us, has gone out from this spot to the ends of the English-speaking world" (Johnson, p. 14).

[Haworth co-indexing entry note]: "John Jacob Niles." Jones, Dorothy, and William E. Studwell. Co-published simultaneously in *Music Reference Services Quarterly* (The Haworth Press, Inc.) Vol. 6, No. 4, 1998, pp. 81-84; and: *Publishing Glad Tidings: Essays on Christmas Music* (William E. Studwell, and Dorothy E. Jones) The Haworth Press, Inc., 1998, pp. 81-84. Single or multiple copies of this article are available for a fee from The Haworth Document Delivery Service [1-800-342-9678, 9:00 a.m. - 5:00 p.m. (EST). E-mail address: getinfo@haworth.com].

John Jacob Niles was born in Louisville, Kentucky, on April 28, 1892. His love for the music of the Appalachian mountain people began when he was a small child. John Thomas Niles, his father, was a farmer, contractor, and sheriff who loved ballads and was himself a good amateur folk singer. He taught John Jacob many ballads and songs, and bought him a three-string dulcimer. Niles said that when he was in his teens and wanted a better instrument, "My father told me to get busy and make one. I've been making my own dulcimers ever since" (*Current Biography* 1959, p. 325). His mother, Lula Sara (Reisch) Niles, was a church organist and a pianist. She taught John Jacob the fundamentals of music, nurturing a love for classical music as well as folk music. John Jacob wrote the wonderful song, "Go 'Way from My Window," when he was in his mid-teens, and when he was over 80 years old, he said: "That tune, I think, did more for my musical awakening than anything I've had to do with. That is, the melodic line and the accompaniment" (Johnson, p. 18).

When he was still in public school, Niles developed a system of musical shorthand and began to keep notes on folk music he heard. He continued this practice while working as a surveyor in various mountain counties. Then came World War I. Niles enlisted as a private in the U.S. Army Air Corps and went to Europe. He served as a ferry pilot, and continued to gather material, taking notes on the songs of men in the fighting units he visited. Niles was severely injured in a plane crash in October 1918, and was discharged with the rank of first lieutenant. He decided to stay in France to study, taking courses at the Université de Lyon and at the Schola Cantorum in Paris. He came home to study at the Cincinnati Conservatory of Music and continued to study and learn throughout his long life, receiving several honorary degrees. Whatever he was doing and wherever he was, he pursued his personal mission to awaken America to its own traditional music. Helen Shea Johnson quotes him: "A national culture is a tenacious thing. . . found in its best and purest form in the arts of the lowliest citizens–that is, the folk-art creations of the nation" (Johnson, p. 14).

While giving concerts during the World War II era, Niles was greatly touched by the effect folk songs had on his concert audiences. Often, people stayed after concerts or sought him out to talk to him about loved ones lost in the war, and to tell him how much his music helped them. In a 1943 article in *Life* magazine, Roger Butterfield noted: "Incidents like these are a great satisfaction to Niles who believes the U.S. has failed seriously to make use of its folk music in wartime. He likes to point out that Germany, Italy, Russia, and England officially encourage the use of folk music to build up a strong national spirit" (Butterfield, p. 58).

Most of Niles's music is music that was handed down, not by notation, but by the informal singing of one generation to the younger members of their families. Niles studied music as an academic discipline, and studied old manuscript collections of songs in the great libraries of the world. His formal study greatly affected his performances and publications. As he walked the mountains, went to village celebrations, and listened to the songs of traveling evangelists, collecting and absorbing music, he sometimes heard songs whose words or ideas were rooted in ancient manuscripts or pictures he had seen in Europe. He found many tunes that had been altered from their original modal form to fit into the more common or popular major-minor scale patterns. Niles usually sang these songs in their original modal form (Butterfield, p. 64). His music generally falls into one of three group-types: folk songs, ballads, and carols. "The folk songs are comparatively new–from 25 to 150 years old–and they deal with familiar subjects like chopping wood and disappointed lovers. . . . The ballads are American versions of English and Scottish ballads about famous people of the 15th and 16th centuries, carried across the Atlantic by early settlers. . . . The carols are the oldest songs of all: they date back to the Middle Ages in England and Europe and deal mostly with domestic events in the life of the Christ Child" (Butterfield, p. 58).

Niles' musical contribution was broad, and Christmas carols comprise a numerically small proportion of his total collection of songs. However, he discovered, or definitively arranged, or made popular, some carols that have taken their place among our best-loved Christmas songs. A sampling of titles is a convincing testimony to how much John Jacob Niles contributed to the enjoyment of all of us who wait expectantly until the Christmas season rolls around so that we can hear the familiar tunes and words that add a special glow to our daily lives. Schirmer's American Folk-Song Series, Set 16, *Ten Christmas Carols from the Southern Appalachian Mountains*, collected and arranged by Niles, contains "Jesus, Jesus, Rest Your Head," "The Seven Joys of Mary," and the wonderfully simple, repeated four-bar setting of "See Jesus the Saviour." Others are not so familiar, such as the lovely, modal "Never Was a Child So Lovely" (*Ballads. . .* , p. 8).

Roger Butterfield tells us about the history of one of John Jacob Niles' most beloved songs, "I Wonder As I Wander:" "Probably the most popular number in Niles's repertoire is a simple little song that has no history at all. One summer afternoon in the small town of Murphy, North Carolina, Niles heard a group of traveling evangelists who had made a 'nuisance' of themselves and had been ordered out of town by sundown. The mayor allowed them to hold one more meeting to raise funds for gasoline. Niles went to the meeting, and there he heard a young girl named Annie Morgan stand up and sing without accompaniment:

I wonder as I wander out under the sky,
How Jesus, our Savior, did come for to die
For poor orn'ry people like you and like I.
I wonder as I wander out under the sky. . .

If Jesus had wanted for any wee thing,
A star in the sky, or a bird on the wing,
Or all of God's angels in Heaven to sing–
He surely could have had it, 'cause he was the King. . .

Niles paid her 25¢ a performance to repeat the four short verses until he had them well written down. Then she and the others drove away, and he has never found any trace of her since. Neither was he able to find in any collection of carols, ancient or modern, anything that even remotely resembled the amazingly beautiful words and music of her song" (Butterfield, p. 60).

REFERENCES

Butterfield, Roger. "Folk Singer," *Life*, Vol. 10 (Sept. 6, 1943), pp. 57-64.
Current Biography Yearbook: 1959, ed. Charles Moritz. New York: H.W. Wilson Company, c. 1959, 1960, pp. 324-26.
Johnson, Helen Shea. "John Jacob Niles: The Minstrel of Boone Creek," *Music Journal*, Jan./Feb. 1980, pp. 13-18.
Niles, John Jacob, comp. *Ballads, Carols and Tragic Legends from the Southern Appalachian Mountains*. New York: G. Schirmer Inc., 1937.
_____ *Ten Christmas Carols from the Southern Appalachian Mountains*. New York: G. Schirmer Inc., 1935.
Thompson, Oscar. *International Cyclopedia of Music and Musicians*, 10th ed., ed. Bruce Bohle. New York: Dodd, Mead, c. 1975.
Who's Who in America 1978-1979, 40th ed., Vol. 2. Chicago: Marquis Who's Who Inc., c. 1978, p. 2404.

Henry W. Simon

Dorothy E. Jones
William E. Studwell

Henry W. Simon edited *A Treasury of Christmas Songs and Carols* in 1955. In his preface he described the unique nature of Christmas songs and his purpose in editing this book. He wrote that "The music of Christmas has a character of its own–so exclusively its own, indeed, that it seems far more absurd to sing Christmas songs out of season than to sing any others throughout the year. By the same token, no other season can boast a literature of song half so rich, half so intimately associated with one time and one time only. . . . Christmas is the time when everyone has always heard music–and the same music. It is the time when people who never sing the rest of the year join in with family groups. . . . It is the family groups that I have had in mind in making the present collection. There are plenty of little paperbound collections of carols, or Christmas sections in hymnals, for the use of more or less formal groups who sing in four parts. But there is not in print, so far as I know, any generous-sized collection of Christmas songs and carols, with big type and gay colors, which will invite the whole family to gather round and peer over local pianists' shoulders as they join in song. . . . I have included all kinds of material, the one criterion being that this is the sort of music people like to sing at Christmas time. I have tried . . . to include all the really universal favorites, a good percentage of those that the ordinary mortal has heard and liked but cannot quite remember the words or tunes to, and a number of comparatively little-known ones from all over the world. A very few have been especially concocted for this book–largely in the last section, 'Rounds and Canons,' the only division for which there was not an embarrassment of riches to select from."

[Haworth co-indexing entry note]: "Henry W. Simon." Jones, Dorothy E., and William E. Studwell. Co-published simultaneously in *Music Reference Services Quarterly* (The Haworth Press, Inc.) Vol. 6, No. 4, 1998, pp. 85-87; and: *Publishing Glad Tidings: Essays on Christmas Music* (William E. Studwell, and Dorothy E. Jones) The Haworth Press, Inc., 1998, pp. 85-87. Single or multiple copies of this article are available for a fee from The Haworth Document Delivery Service [1-800-342-9678, 9:00 a.m. - 5:00 p.m. (EST). E-mail address: getinfo@haworth.com].

The carol book contains a fine selection of the familiar and unfamiliar with historical notes and anecdotes, accompaniments and translations by Henry Simon and his collaborators. Illustrated by Rafaello Busoni, a friend of Simon's, it is a charming book with appeal for both adults and children. The notes following each carol are wonderfully written, like tiny stories, and are testimony to Henry Simon's expertise as an educator and also to a delightful sense of humor. Simon calls these bits of information "gossip," which he includes knowing that "in almost any group there is likely to be at least one fellow who cannot keep a tune and who is best kept busy reading to himself. If they have no other merit, these notes may at least keep him quiet and contented" (Preface). For example, the carol, "A Day of Joy and Feasting," was, according to Simon, concocted out of another carol (also included in the book) by a group of tenth-graders under the leadership of their English and music teachers. In another instance, Simon comments on the "sly humor" of the unusual carol, "Nuns in Frigid Cells," the words of which are from a Henry W. Longfellow poem:

> Nuns in frigid cells
> at this holy tide,
> for want of something else
> Christmas songs at times have tried.
> Let us, by the fire,
> ever, ever higher,
> sing, sing, sing them
> til the night expire. (p. 44)

Henry W. Simon was an educator, music critic, and editor. He was born October 9, 1901, in New York, N.Y., and died there in 1970. He received MA and PhD degrees at Columbia University. After heading the English department at the Fieldston School in New York from 1923 to 1932, he spent eight years as assistant professor of education at his alma mater, Columbia University. During his years at Columbia, he spent one year as an exchange professor of education at Exeter University in England. From 1940 to 1944, he was music critic for the liberal, experimental New York newspaper, *PM*. Then, in 1944, he became vice president and executive editor of Simon and Schuster, the book publishing firm cofounded by his brother. He remained in this position until his retirement in 1967. During these years, he continued his activities as a musicologist, becoming particularly noted for his knowledge of opera and writings in that field. He was also an amateur musician. In discussing the piano accompaniments for his book of carols, which "were designed to give the pianist a bit of fun, too," he says that he and his arranger-collaborator, Rudolph Fellner, "did our best to keep them easy enough for a mediocre pianist without sacrificing musical interest. The test each had to pass was that I had to be able to play it without practicing. That is a pretty severe test; for though I am reasonably fluent with a fiddle, my piano instruction was stopped when as a little boy I showed no talent for the instrument, and I have not practiced since" (Preface).

In 1951, Simon married Rosalind Kunstler and they had a daughter, Patricia. In 1953, he co-edited with Maria Leiper *A Treasury of Hymns*, which contains a section of 41 familiar Christmas carols. Two years later, he produced the lovely *A Treasury of Christmas Songs and Carols*, a popular book albeit carefully indexed, with sources carefully noted and with credit carefully and charmingly given to helpers such as "Lois Friedlander, a first-rate musician who has successfully disguised herself as a most efficient and thoughtful secretary," and to his wife, who "consistently lent courage and cheer at every step" (Preface). This carol book is a fine and fun contribution to the literature of the Christmas carol. It was also, in its time, unusual and creatively conceived for a particular purpose. It was a precursor of the many richly illustrated carol books designed for family unison singing and easy playing that are available on bookstore shelves today.

REFERENCES

Contemporary Authors: A Bio-Bibliographical Guide to Current Authors and Their Works. Vols. 5-8 and 29-32, first revision, cumulated. Detroit, Mich.: Gale Research Company.

Leiper, Maria, and Henry W. Simon, eds. *A Treasury of Hymns*. New York: Simon and Schuster, 1953.

Simon, Henry W., ed. *A Treasury of Christmas Songs and Carols*. Boston: Houghton Mifflin Company, 1955.

Time, Vol. 96, No. 16, p. 74.

Erik Routley

Dorothy E. Jones
William E. Studwell

The January 1983 issue of *Theology Today* carries a final book review by Erik Routley and a memorial statement telling people of his recent death. The memorial is a concise but profound statement of the high esteem in which Routley was held as a scholar, a man, and a Christian.

> We regret to report the death of Erik Routley, Oct. 8, 1982. This book review, so characteristic of his multiple talents and of his literary style, may be the last piece from his hand. A few days before his death, he was busily engaged with a small committee, revising the hymnbook for the Reformed Church of America.
>
> As attested by a steady sequence of definitive volumes, he was by common consent the foremost world authority on church music. An energetic and enthusiastic person, Erik Routley not only knew what he was talking about, but seemed in everything he did to know the joy of his salvation.
>
> On the editor's desk for several weeks, waiting to be properly phrased, lies a scrawled note to invite Erik Routley to prepare a major article for us on the present state of liturgics and church music. Alas, we won't see that article, but we can imagine that Erik is even now taking notes while testing the timbre of the celestial choir. One thing is sure: from now on, worship and praise in Heaven will be of the highest quality. (*Theology Today*, Vol. 39, Jan. 1983, p. 477)

Erik Routley was born in Brighton, Sussex, England, on October 31, 1917, to John and Eleanor Routley. His father was an accountant and his

[Haworth co-indexing entry note]: "Erik Routley." Jones, Dorothy E., and William E. Studwell. Co-published simultaneously in *Music Reference Services Quarterly* (The Haworth Press, Inc.) Vol. 6, No. 4, 1998, pp. 89-93; and: *Publishing Glad Tidings: Essays on Christmas Music* (William E. Studwell, and Dorothy E. Jones) The Haworth Press, Inc., 1998, pp. 89-93. Single or multiple copies of this article are available for a fee from The Haworth Document Delivery Service [1-800-342-9678, 9:00 a.m. - 5:00 p.m. (EST). E-mail address: getinfo@haworth.com].

mother a teacher. He married a music teacher, Margaret Scott, in 1944 and they had three children. He was educated at Magdalen College and Mansfield College, Oxford, receiving his bachelor of divinity in 1943 and his doctorate in 1952. He is described in *Contemporary Authors* (Vol. 108, p. 409) as a clergyman, educator, composer, and author. Ordained a Congregationalist minister in 1943, he served Congregational and United Reformed churches in England and Scotland until 1975. From 1970 to 1971, he was president of the Congregational Church of England and Wales. He was always exceedingly active in worship and church music committees and organizations, accepting offices, lecturing, and publishing. In 1975, he became a professor of church music at Westminster Choir College in Princeton, New Jersey, where he remained until his death. During 1975, he was also visiting professor and director of music at Princeton Theological Seminary.

The purpose of this essay is to highlight Erik Routley's contribution toward the propagation of the Christmas carol. However, interest in the person as well disposes one to look first at the body of his professional work and at the nature of the man revealed therein.

Erik Routley wrote or edited more than 30 books, his subject matter ranging widely through church history, worship, and hymnody. He also published a number of short choral works for church service use. A few of his book titles will give an idea of the expansive nature of his interest and erudition: *Hymns and Human Life*, *The Wisdom of the Fathers*, *The Gift of Conversion*, *English Religious Dissent*, *Twentieth-Century Church Music*, *The Organist's Guide to Congregational Praise*. Many people have multiple interests, but it takes a special kind of scholarship, wit, skill, and perception to write about all of them.

Routley wrote one book entitled *The Puritan Pleasures of the Detective Story* (London: Victor Gollanz Ltd., 1972). The preface offers insight into Erik Routley's character, which included a wonderful sense of humor and a personal security that enabled him to laugh at himself and to thoroughly enjoy living. Routley describes a much-loved Old Testament scholar who read detective stories voraciously. He "had a most enviable library of them, collected over a long period. He knew the literature as intimately as he knew the Pentateuch. But he would not have written this book." Comparing himself to the biblical scholar, Routley says: "Having far less to lose than he in the matter of reputation for zeal and high seriousness, I am now allowing myself an indulgence which I have long promised myself—a record of what I read in bed. Some friends will be ashamed to acknowledge me after this: for what will often have appeared to them as a slightly frivolous mind will now manifest itself as an irretrievably trivial one."

Routley made a significant contribution to the literature about the Christmas carol. He edited the *University Carol Book* in 1961. Approximately 50% of the collection is made up of "Nativity carols." Routley is cited in Studwell's *Christmas Carols: A Reference Guide* as the composer of the music for two carols, "The Cedar of Lebanon" and "The Sinners' Redemption" (Studwell, pp. 39 and 190). If you look at the entire body of Routley's writings and compositions, his work on carols looks very minor indeed. However, Erik Routley wrote a wonderful book entitled *The English Carol*. He begins it with the words, "I do not know that there could be a more delightful task than that which the publisher invited me to undertake in preparing this book about carols. . . ." He defined his purpose in writing the book: "My own purpose is to tell the story of carol-singing, and place it over against church history, in much the same way which I have ventured to adopt with hymns and their tunes" (Preface, p. 7). The book is a scholarly examination of the history of English carols. Yet it always manages to be fun to read. Routley leans heavily on *The Oxford Book of Carols*, and *The English Carol* actually serves as a fine narrative companion to that classic collection. Routley helps clarify the difference between various types of Christmas songs that we tend to label *en masse* as carols. "Once in royal David's city" was one of a series of hymns written to explain the catechism to children; "It came upon the midnight clear" is "not a Nativity hymn in any sense, but a hymn exhorting men to follow the way of peace." "O little town of Bethlehem" is "a shade too poetically contrived, too self-conscious . . . to pass as a genuine carol" (pp. 160-62).

Routley divides his book into three parts, each containing three chapters. Part One, "The Singing Ages," deals with medieval manuscript carols, then with ballads. Part Two, entitled "The Great Controversy," contains a discussion of late-medieval processions and drama, their encounters with the Puritan mind, and the shift from carols to hymns. Part Three, "The Return of the Carol," has a chapter on 19th-century social and religious developments as they influenced carols, a chapter on carols from other countries, and a chapter on 20th-century carols, carol singing, and services.

At the very beginning of his book, Routley quotes Percy Dearmer's definition of carols: "Carols are songs with a religious impulse that are simple, hilarious, popular, and modern" (*The Oxford Book of Carols*, p. v). In his introduction to the *University Carol Book*, he says: "A carol is, in its most ancient meaning, not a song but a dance, not a religious but a secular act" (p. v). At the end of his book, *The English Carol*, Routley says:

> If Christmas is the season especially of the putting down of the mighty from their seat, then Christmas is the archetypal carol season. A whole tradition of heresy is based on the notion that the Incarnation is a humiliation unworthy of the Eternal God. It survives today in that tight-lipped stoicism that cannot admit the ridiculous into life because it dare not admit the redeemability of life. "The genius of the present age requires work and not play." Work is what you do in the firm's time. Work is good, it is good for you, it is not to be treated lightly. And what was the work of God? To create the world in all its majestic design, and then to rescue it from frustration and grievance by an undignified act that begins with an impromptu cradle in a cowshed and ends with the gross horror of a crucifixion. Where that becomes not remote dogma but a texture of life, where men see that reality is as terrible and as triumphant as that, there you lose at once the cautious speech of the man of worldly weight, the portentous demeanor of the reputable and respected, and you get something like a "general dance" In a word, you get carols. (p. 242)

Routley's analysis of the message of the carol embodies, it seems to me, the message of Erik Routley's life–a devotion and commitment, full of joy and free, refusing to take things so seriously that hilarity and fun are abstracted from faith, the most joyous part of our lives.

REFERENCES

Contemporary Authors: A Bio-Bibliographical Guide to Current Writers in Fiction, General Nonfiction, Poetry, Journalism, Drama, Motion Pictures, Television and Other Fields, Vol. 5, Ann Evory, ed. Detroit, Mich.: Gale Research Company.

Contemporary Authors: A Bio-Bibliographical Guide to Current Writers in Fiction, General Nonfiction, Poetry, Journalism, Drama, Motion Pictures, Television, and Other Fields, Vol. 108, Hal May: ed. Detroit, Mich: Gale Research Company.

Dearmer, Percy et al., *The Oxford Book of Carols.* Oxford University Press: London, 1928.

Routley, Erik, A review of *Liturgies and Trials: The Secularization of Religious Language,* by Richard K. Fenn in *Theology Today,* Vol. 39, No. 4 (Jan, 1983), pp. 475-77.

Routley, Erik, *The English Carol.* London: Herbert Jenkins, 1958.

Routley, Erik, ed., *University Carol Book: A Collection of Carols from Many Lands, for All Seasons.* London: H. Freeman & Co., 1961.

Studwell, William E., *Christmas Carols: A Reference Guide.* New York: Garland Publishing Company, 1985.

George K. Evans

Dorothy E. Jones
William E. Studwell

George K. Evans's name is not found in those books that list and immortalize our more famous citizens, but he was a prime mover in the creation of one of the more imaginative and unusual Christmas carol books produced during the 20th century. He, along with Walter Ehret, edited *The International Book of Christmas Carols*, published by Prentice-Hall Inc. in 1963. The book was reprinted by S. Greene Press in 1980. George Evans is credited with doing most of the translations and the notes, both of which are essential to the unique character and high quality of the book. It is a very attractive carol collection, with a profusion of black and white illustrations by Don Martinetti, and with a most complimentary foreword by Norman Luboff. The settings for the carols, most of which were arranged by Walter Ehret, are simple, as are the accompaniments, and each carol falls into a comfortable voice range. Chord symbols are included with each carol, and near the end of the book there is a guitar-chord chart, adapted from *Tennessee Ernie Ford's Book of Favorite Hymns* (1962). However, more than anything else, it is one of the first truly international carol books, containing tunes and words from many countries and many historic periods, carefully giving equal emphasis to the texts in their original languages and in English. The translations fit each tune very well, so that the original rhythmic movement of the carol is not disturbed. Norman Luboff states that "There are a great many [carols] which have not previously appeared in any collection. The Slavic, Scandinavian, and Spanish carols are particularly noteworthy in this respect."

The International Book of Christmas Carols was published during a

[Haworth co-indexing entry note]: "George K. Evans." Jones, Dorothy E., and William E. Studwell. Co-published simultaneously in *Music Reference Services Quarterly* (The Haworth Press, Inc.) Vol. 6, No. 4, 1998, pp. 95-97; and: *Publishing Glad Tidings: Essays on Christmas Music* (William E. Studwell, and Dorothy E. Jones) The Haworth Press, Inc., 1998, pp. 95-97. Single or multiple copies of this article are available for a fee from The Haworth Document Delivery Service [1-800-342-9678, 9:00 a.m. - 5:00 p.m. (EST). E-mail address: getinfo@haworth.com].

time of intense awareness of the need for an ecumenical Christian community. It was also a time when concentrated efforts were made to soften or erase national barriers so that mankind could work together to make the world a better place for all. Language study was a requirement in the curriculum of more and more high schools. Foreign language study was a prerequisite for entrance into many colleges and universities as well as being an essential part of the college curriculum. *The International Book of Christmas Carols* was truly a book of the early '60s. Arms stretched across oceans and international activities were accompanied by a sense of joy, purpose, and excited anticipation of a future we thought we could mold. Right and wrong seemed to be more clearly discernible to most individuals then than now. Many of us were activists with a sense of hope. We had not quite begun our journey to the '90s, during which we became a confused people, bewildered by a complicated emotional mixture of horrors and pleasures, trust and suspicion, fear, cynicism, hope, and futility. Reading George Evans's preface to the carol book makes one acutely aware of the bright hope of the early '60s–what some would call a naive belief that if we understood each other, we would all live together in peace and harmony; and we believed then that it surely could not be too difficult to understand one another. This belief is somewhat shaken now, but not yet dead; and it is at Christmastime that the bright hope glows again. The easy accessibility of the carols in this collection, and the obvious consciousness of the importance of every nation's contribution, can help rekindle the little fire that guards hope for our future.

George Evans wrote a fine seven-page introductory essay entitled "Christmas and Its Songs." He traces the flowing history of Christmas-festival customs and moods, from their roots in Sumerian civilization through Mesopotamian celebrations and Roman sun-worship practices of the Saturnalia festival to the influence of the Celtic god Woden with his wonderful eight-legged horse. Then, "In this pagan setting Christ made his appearance. His birthdate was hardly noted for some time, even by Christians. To them, the Resurrection was the important thing, and they expected him to return any day" (p. 2). But gradually, as the Christian faith spread, more people became curious about the date of Christ's birth and wanted to celebrate his coming. Converts often wanted to observe their old rituals as well as those of Christianity. So old celebrations were gradually Christianized, adapted, and absorbed. Old ribaldry was toned down and early-Christian ascetic severity was softened. The festival of Christmas was gradually being developed. Legends of Nicholas, Archbishop of Myra, spread and the traits of Nicholas became mixed with those of Woden. Evans writes of Jewish temple hymns, secular songs from

Greek plays, and songs sung in medieval mystery plays. Thus George Evans helps us understand the composite nature of our own celebration and the synthesis of cultures and customs that produced our festival and our carols.

Our world is still shrinking at a great rate, and our present-day news reports regularly force us to become cognizant of the activities, happenings, and conditions in places we used to think of as obscure. *The International Book of Carols* contains carols from the Western world and will not, therefore, come close to global representation. However, it was widely inclusive for its time: 52 English carols (British, American, etc.); 28 German (e.g., Austrian, Dutch); 27 Spanish; 19 French; 19 Slavic; 10 Scandinavian; 4 Italian; 5 Latin.

George Evans's notes on the individual carols are included on pages 320 through 329 of the book. The notes are alphabetized by title, using the title in the original language. The index of first lines at the very end of the book contains the first lines of each carol in both the original language and the English translation. Evans's notes are informative little paragraphs on the facts and legends adhering to each carol, and are a very helpful resource for gaining an understanding of the carols.

Most of us are very familiar with *The Oxford Book of Carols*, first published by the Oxford University Press in 1928, and widely accepted as a classic collection. We are less familiar with *The International Book of Christmas Carols*, which is stylistically different and more limited in scope, containing only carols of the Christmas season. *The International Book of Christmas Carols* is an enlightened and aesthetically pleasing collection of carols, also worthy to be called a classic.

William E. Studwell

Dorothy E. Jones

William E. Studwell's book, *Christmas Carols: A Reference Guide*, was published in 1985 and is, to date, the most complete bibliography of Christmas carols available. This book was the culmination and consolidation of two major forces in Mr. Studwell's life: (1) a love of music which was an extension of his love of hymns heard over and over during his childhood and young adult years, and (2) his professional interest, as a librarian, in bibliography and cataloging.

Born in Stamford, Connecticut, on March 18, 1936, William "Bill" Studwell was the seventh child of a lower middle-class working family. His mother had a high-school education and worked in a factory; his father had a grammar-school education, worked as a carpenter and in other varied jobs, and was not a supporter of education. It was his mother who nurtured his intellectual growth and who encouraged him to go to college.

Studwell graduated from Stamford High School in 1954 and attended the Stamford branch of the University of Connecticut for two years. From 1956 to 1959, he was enrolled at the University of Connecticut in the small town of Storrs, which then had no bar, no bowling alley, no bank, and no theater. He majored in history, developed an interest in sports, and continued his studies after his BA to take a master's degree in European history in 1959. He was most interested in cultural history, an interest that continues today and is reflected in his writings. Studwell worked during all of his years in college, and after graduation continued to do various odd jobs until, in 1962, he landed a minor position with a government agency and went to Washington, D.C. It was not long before he transferred to the Library of Congress where, because he could speak and read Russian

[Haworth co-indexing entry note]: "William E. Studwell." Jones, Dorothy E. Co-published simultaneously in *Music Reference Services Quarterly* (The Haworth Press, Inc.) Vol. 6, No. 4, 1998, pp. 99-101; and: *Publishing Glad Tidings: Essays on Christmas Music* (William E. Studwell, and Dorothy E. Jones) The Haworth Press, Inc., 1998, pp. 99-101. Single or multiple copies of this article are available for a fee from The Haworth Document Delivery Service [1-800-342-9678, 9:00 a.m. - 5:00 p.m. (EST). E-mail address: getinfo@haworth.com].

moderately well, he found a niche in the technical division of their Soviet and Russian collection. He quickly began taking classes in the Library School at Catholic University in Washington, continuing to work full-time, and received his MSLS (Master of Library Science) degree in 1967. In 1966, he became a classification specialist in the Dewey Decimal Division of the library, where he worked until 1968. From 1968 to 1970, he headed a small community college library in Roscommon, Michigan. In 1970, he accepted a position as head cataloger at the University Libraries, Northern Illinois University (NIU), in DeKalb, Illinois. He is now principal cataloger at NIU, and, in September 1990, was honored as the most published library journal article author among academic librarians during the years 1983 to 1987. In 1992, he was given a lifetime achievement plaque for extensive publication and outstanding service by the Illinois Association of College and Research Libraries.

Bill Studwell has always loved hymns and carols. His was a conservative, fundamentalist Christian family, and the church was at the center of family life. He had a liking for some popular tunes, but had no interest in classical music at all. Then, in the late '50s, his brother Alfred, who later became a physician, introduced Bill to his classical music record collection. Bill scoffed at his brother's taste in music, but listened anyway and discovered he loved classical music. He began listening to classics stations on the radio. One of his favorite pieces was the overture to the ballet *Sylvia*, by Leo Delibes. He began researching Delibes and also became interested in the music of Delibes' composition teacher, Adolphe Adam, a French composer best known for his operas and ballets. (Adolphe Adam composed the melody for the Christmas carol, "O Holy Night.")

Much later, in 1987, Studwell was to write a book, *Adolphe Adam and Leo Delibes: A Guide to Research*, which was published by Garland in the Garland Composer Resource Manuals series. Two other books grew out of his interest in ballet and opera: *Opera Plot Index*, coauthored with David Hamilton (Garland, 1990), and *Ballet Plot Index* (Garland, 1987). The latter was honored as one of *Choice Magazine's* "Outstanding Academic Books of 1988/1989." The enduring nature of Bill's interests and the way in which one enthusiasm led naturally to others are illustrated in his publishing record. Like Adolphe Adam, who according to *The New Grove Dictionary of Music and Musicians* (Vol. 1, p. 91) was a "prolific composer who wrote music with extreme facility," Studwell writes easily and often. By 1993, he had published over ten books and approximately 200 articles. Interestingly, his writing and publishing all began with a little pamphlet he produced as a Christmas present. In 1965, William had married Ann Stroia, whom he met while in Washington. Ann's family drew names for Christmas gifts in 1972, and all the participants were to make a gift for the person whose name they drew. William didn't have an interest in crafts, so he decided he would write a pamphlet about Adolphe Adam and "O Holy Night." He was pleased with the result and continued to write, publishing an article on carols in the *Journal of Church Music* in 1976, and then writing an article on 19th-and early-20th century ballet that was published in *Dance Scope* (Vol. 10, No. 2: 51-55, Spring 1976).

Studwell is very much interested in collecting Christmas carols, in telling people about them, and in helping to expand the carol repertoire beyond the few old favorites. Besides writing prolifically on the subject, he has made many presentations on radio and television and has lectured before local groups. His more than 40 articles on Christmas carols include "The Cultural Impact of the Christmas Carol" *Journal of Church Music* 24, No. 10: 13-14, December 1982); "Bach and the Christmas Carol" (*The American Organist* 20, No. 11: 26, November 1986); a series of articles on the history of particular carols, published in *The American Organist*, 1988-90; and a series entitled "Obscure Carol Classics," which he coauthored and published in *The Choral Journal* in 1988. Although he has published books in the field of library cataloging, the majority of his books concern music. He contributed the text to Hal Leonard's 1991 book, *The Christmas Card Songbook*, and has another book on carols, *A Christmas Carol Reader*, which he expects to have published soon. *Christmas Carols: A Reference Guide*, mentioned at the beginning of this article, is a historical dictionary of carols from around the world. Each entry contains notes on the author, composer, place of origin, date of origin, and at least one publication in which the carol can be found. The bibliography is extensive and it is indexed by title, person and group, and place. It is a very rich resource.

Oddly enough, Studwell's most productive years have been from 1982 through the present, the same period that has encompassed a serious deterioration of his health. His enthusiasm and determination, however, remain intact and I expect that we will see further additions to his large and significant contributions to the literature of the Christmas carol.

(The sources for this article were personal interviews with William Studwell during the summer of 1994, acquaintance with his publications, and my own knowledge of him as a colleague over a period of eleven years.)

OBSCURE CAROL CLASSICS

Obscure Carol Classics I:
Charles Hutchins'
Carols Old and Carols New

William E. Studwell
Dorothy Jones

I. HISTORICAL BACKGROUND

By William E. Studwell

In 1916 a monumental collection of carols was published. This work, with the title page reading "Carols Old and Carols New: For Use at Christmas and Other Seasons of the Christian Year, collected from many sources and arranged by the Rev. Charles L. Hutchins," was issued by the Parish Choir, Boston. It was an enormous volume, clothbound, preface, xvii, 659 pages, with 751 carols, three good indexes (authors, translators, and sources of texts; composers and sources of music; first line index, by season), a four page bibliography which included many unusual and older items, and some data on the authorship of the carols. About 63% of the carols were for Christmas, about 27% were for Easter, and about 10% were for Ascension/Whitsun-tide, Harvest-time, Children's Day, and Flower Services. Some of the carols had been issued previously in the

---

William E. Studwell and Dorothy Jones, "Obscure Carol Classics I: Charles Hutchins' *Carols Old and Carols New*," *Choral Journal 29* (August 1988): 11-14. © 1988 by the American Choral Directors Association, P.O. Box 6310, Lawton, Oklahoma 73506-0310. U.S.A. Used by permission.

[Haworth co-indexing entry note]: "Obscure Carol Classics I: Charles Hutchins' *Carols Old and Carols New*." Studwell, William E., and Dorothy Jones. Co-published simultaneously in *Music Reference Services Quarterly* (The Haworth Press, Inc.) Vol. 6, No. 4, 1998, pp. 105-113; and: *Publishing Glad Tidings: Essays on Christmas Music* (William E. Studwell, and Dorothy E. Jones) The Haworth Press, Inc., 1998, pp. 105-113. Single or multiple copies of this article are available for a fee from The Haworth Document Delivery Service [1-800-342-9678, 9:00 a.m. - 5:00 p.m. (EST). E-mail address: getinfo@haworth.com].

Parish Choir, a serial published from 1874 to c. 1919 and also edited by Hutchins (1838-1920).

Many of the carols in this international collection are well-known, but many are uncommon or unique. In addition, some of the better-known carols are printed with texts or tunes which are in some way unusual. For example, the first printing of the English translation *Angels We Have Heard on High* in its present form (which is quite different from the 1862 original) may have been in this volume. Its contents, therefore, are substantially unique. Furthermore, in scope and comprehensiveness it is also unique. It is the largest known one-volume collection ever gathered in an English-speaking country, and it is unique in yet another way: it has the best accompanying material (historical data, indexes, and bibliography) of any English language collection prior to the *Oxford Book of Carols* (*1928*).

In size and accompanying material *Carols Old and Carols New* far surpasses all other pre-*Oxford Book* collections. Bramley and Stainer's ca. 1878 second edition has only 70 carols and relatively little other data. Chope's 1894 second edition (215 carols) is much larger than Bramley and Stainer but still is considerably smaller than *Carols Old* and has relatively little other data. Yet Bramley and Stainer and Chope are much better-known than *Carols Old*. The cause of this relative obscurity is twofold. First, only 1,000 copies of *Carols Old* were printed in comparison to the mass marketing of the other two collections. Second, only twelve years after *Carols Old* appeared, the superlative *Oxford Book of Carols* was issued thereby eclipsing what fame a limited edition publication could generate. Yet despite fine later collections such as *Oxford Book*, Henry Simon's *Christmas Songs and Carols* (1955), Erik Routley's *University Carol Book* (1961), and *The International Book of Carols* (1963), *Carols Old* still has much to offer.

II. COMMENTARY ON THE MUSIC

By Dorothy Jones

Charles Hutchins, compiler of *Carols Old and Carols New*, declares the purpose of his massive collection in the preface (p. iii):

> The excuse, if any be needed, for the publication of this collection of carols, is a double one: viz., the happy and widely prevailing return in recent years to the old custom of carol singing, and the desire on the part of the compiler to further this custom by placing within the reach of those who engage in it, an abundance of good materials.

Although Hutchins states that "none are here reprinted which have not, at least in one circle, attained some degree of popularity" (preface, p. iii), the collection is a book of its time and necessarily contains a fair amount of music of little long-term value. Many carols are harmonized with the trite and predictable progressions and cadences popular for gospel tunes of the late nineteenth and early twentieth centuries. As an example, one might look at Carol No. 459, "The Stars are Brightly Shining." The chord progressions are sentimental, chromatic, and predictable. This carol was chosen at random by the authors and is similar in character to many that were sung and enjoyed enormously during this period of church history. They remind one of old familiar hymns such as "Living for Jesus" (music by C. Harold Lowden; copyright 1917 by The Heidelberg Press) or "Make Somebody Happy Today" (music by Charles H. Gabriel; copyright 1915 by Homer A. Rodeheaver).

However, there are also a few rare jewels and a great many very pleasant melodies tucked away in this collection, with lyrics that are poetically worthy, and theologically interesting. Emphases within Christian theological circles go in and out of fashion and favor, but the bits and pieces of thought and inspiration that form our theology seldom disappear completely. The myriad thoughts and convictions of the faith are still extant somewhere among our denominations and sects and are quite likely to surface again sometime. Remnants of almost all theological and credal concepts can be found somewhere in the words of our hymns and carols. If, for example, you feel that it might be a healthy thing for a bit of guilt and repentance to surface again, you might want to use the beautiful song "Remember, O Thou Man" (Carol No. 705). The first verse reads:

Remember O thou man,
O thou man, O thou man,
Remember, O thou man,
Thy time is spent:
Remember, O thou man,
How thou art dead and gone,
And I did what I can, Therefore repent.

(Words from "Melismata," 1611. Tune by Thomas Ravenscroft.)

If you are a choral director looking for something new for your Service of Scripture and Carols during the Christmas season, locate *Carols Old and Carols New* in a library and build a service around some of the lovely, interesting carols found there that are very difficult, if not impossible, to find elsewhere. I chose the following group of ten and, in the process, found enough to keep me supplied with new carols for many Christmases.

CONCERNING THE SHEPHERDS

Carol No. 413: "A Shepherd Band their Flocks," by Praetorius, 1609.

This is a rich and rhythmically interesting chorale. Written here in 4/4 time, it is easy for a choir to read, but manages, by means of the use of fermatas and rests, to feel unmetered or, at least, irregular. The words fit the tune very well, both emotionally and rhythmically (Example 1).

Carol No. 562: "Shepherds Watching O'er the Plain," by Edwin Lemare. Words by Mrs. A. Gaskell.

This is a delicate and peaceful little carol. The whole carol, and particularly measures 8 through 11, is evocative of the song-style of the late nineteenth century (Example 2).

EXAMPLE 1

Through field and wood the song resoundeth,
O'er hill and vale the chorus boundeth :
Exultingly the echoes roll,
And hymns of triumph spread from pole to pole.

6
The shepherds view the host returning,
Their hearts with holy ardour burning;
To Bethlehem they wend their way,
Repeating with glad tongues th' angelic lay.

7
In haste they seek the heavenly Stranger ;
They find the Babe laid in a manger ;
With wonder and with awe they fall,
And joyfully adore Him, Lord of all.

8
Now every voice with rapture swelleth,
For Christ the Lord with mortals dwelleth ;
Let men and angels Him adore,
And shout their loud hosannas evermore.

AT THE MANGER

Carol No. 182: "Infant So Gentle," a Gascon carol.

This short and simple lullaby, depending harmonically on the I, IV, and V chords, could be sung chorally in four parts and repeated in unison by children or soloist. As a unison song, it seems to invite accompaniment by autoharp or guitar.

Carol No. 27: "Sleep, My Saviour, Sleep," Bohemian, arr. by Rev. R. F. Smith. Words by the Rev. S. Baring-Gould.

The tune of this gentle lullaby may be familiar to some readers. Exactly repeated chords give the carol a rocking, lulling, childlike character. This carol could be treated in the same manner as Carol No. 182 (Example 3).

JOURNEY OF THE KINGS

Carol No. 464: "O'er the Hill and O'er the Vale," tune "in vernali tempore" harmonized by Rev. G.R. Woodward. Words by Dr. John Mason Neale.

The words of this carol make one aware of the all-encompassing spaciousness of the Christmas story and its implications for the world. The straight quarter-note $^6_4$ rhythm of the first line, together with the melodic progression (a step, then a skip of a third, and this repeated:

gives the first line a feeling of bumpy camel travel. The strong $^6_4$ rhythmic emphasis (♩♩♩♩) in the first measure of the second line sets this section apart and, in combination with the words, emphasizes the adventurousness and vision of the three kings (Example 4).

Carol No. 465: "O'er Bethlehem's Hill in Time of Old," by A. E. Floyd. Words by M. G. Pearse.

This happy, dancing, little tune is written as a unison carol with accompaniment underneath. The words do not always fit the rhythm of the melody perfectly.

EXAMPLE 2

Carol 562. Shepherds watching o'er the plain.
CHRISTMAS.
Words by *Mrs. Gaskell.*   *Edwin Lemare.*

Allegro moderato.

mf

1. Shep - herds watch.ing o'er the plain, Tell us what ye heard, Whis - per of the
2. Shep - herds, ye who saw the light Through the riv - en clouds, Tell us of that

rall.

glad re - frain That your bos - oms stirr'd.
won-drous night Ye in fear were bowed.

3
Tell us, shepherds, what ye saw
When the guiding star
Led ye to a bed of straw
In a cave afar!

4
Tell us of a Mother meek,
Of a Babe divine;
Tell us, show us, where to seek
That most holy shrine.

Parish Choir, No. 1789 — 4.   446

THE CHRISTMAS STORY FOR THE MODERN WORLD

Carol No. 469: "Gather Around the Christmas Tree," by Rev. J. H. Hopkins.

This is a joyful song of celebration with the Christmas tree a Christian symbol. The tune and harmony are catchy, though not especially memorable, but the words are unusual. They bring into the service the idea of the Christmas tree, which is certainly a central symbol of Christmas in most of the homes of the congregation.

Carol No. 10: "Slowly Fall the Snowflakes," by W. Borrow. Words by Rev. F. G. Lee.

The words of this carol describe Christmas in a snowy setting, with the white snow a symbol of the Virgin. The musical setting is a simple, straightforward hymn tune in four-part harmony.

EXAMPLE 3

Sleep, my Saviour, sleep.

Carol 27.   (FOR CHRISTMAS.)   *Bohemian. Arranged by Rev. R. F. Smith.*

Sleep, my Sav-iour, sleep, On Thy bed of hay; An-gels in the span-gled Heaven Sing their gladsome Christ-mas car-ols Till the dawn of day.

2
Sleep, my SAVIOUR, sleep,
On Thy bed of hay,
Ere the mourning Angel cometh
To the moon-lit olive garden,
Wiping tears away.

3
Sleep, my SAVIOUR, sleep,
Sweet on Mary's breast,
Now the shepherds kneel adoring,
Now the mother's heart is joyous,
Take a happy rest.

4
Sleep, my SAVIOUR, sleep,
Sweet on Mary's breast,
Crucified, with wounds and bruises
Bleeding, purple, stained, disfigured,
One day Thou wilt rest.

EXAMPLE 4

O'er the hill and o'er the vale.

Carol 464.   CHRISTMAS AND EPIPHANY.   Tune "*In vernali tempore.*"
Words by *Dr. John Mason Neale.*   Har. by *Rev. G. R. Woodward.*

1. { O'er the hill and o'er the vale, Come three kings to-geth-er, }
{ Car-ing nought for snow and hail, Cold and wind and wea-ther; }

{ Now on Per-sia's sand-y plains, Now where Ti-gris swells with rains, They their cam-els te-ther: }
{ Now thro' Syrian lands they go, Now thro' Mo-ab, faint and slow, Now o'er Edom's hea-ther. }

2 O'er the hill and o'er the vale,
Each king bears a present:
Wise men go a Child to hail,
Monarchs seek a Peasant:
And a star in front proceeds,
Over rocks and rivers leads,
Shines with beams incessant:
Therefore onward, onward still!
Ford the stream and climb the hill:
Love makes all things pleasant.

3 He is God ye go to meet:
Therefore incense proffer:
He is King ye go to greet;
Gold is in your coffer:
Also Man, He comes to share
Ev'ry woe that man can bear—
Tempter, Railer, Scoffer:
Therefore now, against the day,
In the grave when Him they lay,
Myrrh ye also offer.

THE CHRISTMAS STORY PROCLAIMED

Carol No. 18: "Now Lift the Carol, Men and Maids," by Arthur H. Brown. Words by Rev. A. M. Morgan.

This carol consists of words of proclamation set to a gay and dancelike tune in verse-chorus form. It is suitable for either unison or part-singing. The three verses tell the story in a quick, light, spritely $\frac{6}{8}$ rhythm which consists mostly of the pattern: 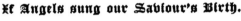. The chorus is heavier and suggests, both by the change in rhythmic emphasis and the repetition of the "Noel," a freer, more abandoned style of singing to emulate a shout of joy.

Carol No. 21: "If Angels Sung our Savior's Birth," by Arthur H. Brown.

This chorale expresses the totality of the Jesus story from Christmas through Easter. Strong and joyous in character, the running eighth notes in all parts make this fun to sing in parts even though it is suggested as a "treble solo." The chorus is sung in Latin, which adds to the fun of singing it and to the sense of history implicit in the words (Example 5).

EXAMPLE 5

4.
Then, with perpetual hymns, let Christ,
Who from the dead was raised,
With Father and the Holy Ghost,
Eternally be praised.

CHORUS. AFTER EACH VERSE.

Sur - rex - it Chris-tus ho - di - e, Sur - rex - it pro no - - - bis; Sur-

After the last verse.
Slow.

rex - it Chris-tus ho - di - e, Glo - ria Je - su Dom - i - no. Al - - - le - lu - ia!

Parish Choir, No. 56 — 4.

21

Obscure Carol Classics II:
Richard Terry's *Two Hundred Folk Carols*

William E. Studwell
Dorothy Jones

I. HISTORICAL BACKGROUND

By William E. Studwell

Sir Richard Runciman Terry (1865-1938) was one of the key figures in the history of Christmas carols. In addition to an impressive list of other works, which he wrote, edited, or arranged, he produced three books on carols which could well be regarded as classics. He published two of these in 1931, *Gilbert and Sandys' Christmas Carols* (London: Burns, Oates & Washbourne), a small but extremely competent study of the two early carol collections, and *A Medieval Carol Book* (London: Burns, Oates & Washbourne), again a small volume but one of the most important collections of medieval carols.

The third classic, *Two Hundred Folk Carols* (London: Burns, Oates & Washbourne), was published in 1933. THF was just as well done as the other two, but is especially valuable because of its size and scope. It has a preface, xxxii, 395 pages, and contains sixty-eight English carols, eighteen French carols, ten Besançon carols, eleven Bernaise and Burgundian carols, thirteen Provençal carols, eighteen Basque carols, nineteen Dutch and

William E. Studwell and Dorothy Jones, "Obscure Carol Classics II: Richard Terry's *Two Hundred Folk Carols*," *Choral Journal 29* (September 1988): 19-22. ©1988 by the American Choral Directors Association, P.O. Box 6310, Lawton, Oklahoma 73506-0310. U.S.A. Used by permission.

[Haworth co-indexing entry note]: "Obscure Carol Classics II: Richard Terry's *Two Hundred Folk Carols*." Studwell, William E., and Dorothy Jones. Co-published simultaneously in *Music Reference Services Quarterly* (The Haworth Press, Inc.) Vol. 6, No. 4, 1998, pp. 115-123; and: *Publishing Glad Tidings: Essays on Christmas Music* (William E. Studwell, and Dorothy E. Jones) The Haworth Press, Inc., 1998, pp. 115-123. Single or multiple copies of this article are available for a fee from The Haworth Document Delivery Service [1-800-342-9678, 9:00 a.m. - 5:00 p.m. (EST). E-mail address: getinfo@haworth.com].

Flemish carols, ten Italian carols, twenty-one German, Alsatian, and Polish carols, twelve European medieval carols, and two good indexes. The songs are all in English, with the title of all foreign carols given and the texts of the Latin carols and one Italian carol also printed. Some of the carols are well known, such as *The First Nowell, God Rest Ye Merry, Gentlemen, Patapan, Good King Wenceslas, Lo How a Rose, and Puer natus in Bethlehem,* but most are lesser known and a number are comparatively rare and/or quaint. Among the unusual titles are *Cheer Up, Old Woman, The Laundry Carol, The Weather Carol, There Came a Shy Intruder, O Hinds Tune Up Your Pipes,* and *The Gossoon and the Gaffer Carol.*

The carols were published in ten separately-paged groups, and six of these sections (Basque; Bernaise and Burgundian; Dutch and Flemish; German, Alsatian, and Polish; Italian; Provençal) were issued individually at about the same time. This double publication is one indicator of the interest in these carols two generations ago, and combined with the publication of a number of the uncommon carols in Erik Routley's *University Carol Book* (1961) one generation ago, suggests that Terry's collection may still be of much value today. In size it is the largest known collection in the English language devoted entirely to folk material. In character it is quite unusual because of the substantial number of carols from lesser-treated areas like the Basque region, the Besançon region, Burgundy, Provence, and Italy. In quality it has few peers, mainly because of the skill and devotion of Sir Richard Runciman Terry.

II. COMMENTARY ON THE MUSIC

By Dorothy Jones

Sir Richard Terry describes the purpose of his collection of folk carols in his preface (p. vii):

> This collection has been primarily compiled for the use of choirs, but it cannot be too strongly emphasized that all the carols–save the definitely polyphonic ones (e.g., those of Praetorius)–can be effectively sung as solos, or by voices in unison, with or *without* accompaniment. The bulk of them are folk-melodies, and should be treated as such. Even the carols of Praetorius are simple harmonizations of popular melodies.

We might look at the Basque carol, No. 96, "In middle winter they set out." This is a good example of a carol arranged specifically for a choir.

Two-part treble voices sing the words most of the time, accompanied by a tenor/bass hum. However, the carol would also be very nice sung in a free tempo by a soloist, or sung in unison by choir or congregation (Example 1).

The consistent excellence of quality of the carols is particularly notable. Some of the tunes are familiar. For example, carol No. 99 (or page 16 in the Basque carol section) with the words "We Sing of David's Daughter," is the same tune as No. 159, or "Sing to the Lord of Harvest" in the *Oxford Book of Carols*. But many of the carols are rare or seldom-heard songs. Some of the carols which seem most quaint and amusing to us are those like the Provençal Noel, "The Gouty Carol," No. 80 (Example 2). It combines the mundane and the holy in a humorous song of regret by a gentleman whose gouty leg prevents him from joining in a pilgrimage in honor of the birth of Christ. According to Sir Richard Terry, "The words of this carol would appear to have been highly popular judging by the number of tunes with which they are associated" (p. 4 of Part V: Provençal Carols). The tune here presented is charming, and extremely simple, since the first three measures of every four-measure phrase consist of the same melody pattern.

Quite a few of the carol tunes have irregular phrase lengths and free-feeling lines which make them interesting and lovely for choral presentation and may partially account for their unfamiliarity among modern-day carol singers. Look for example at No. 126, the Dutch melody "The World Has Waited Long" (Example 3). We have a tendency to want our music in neat four-bar phrases. However, the first phrase of this carol is stretched to five measures, giving the singer a sense of going beyond normal boundaries, and structurally illustrating the words, "waited long."

The translations of the words are, almost without exception, pleasing when read aloud as poetry and fit the tunes with elegant precision. One is hard put to find examples of those awkwardnesses so often found in lyric translations where the emphases of the spoken line pull against the stress of the melodic phrase. Richard Terry writes about himself, as overseer of the translation process, in the preface, p. viii:

> As regards the translations of the Latin, French, and German carols his librettists have gone direct to the original texts. In the case of old Dutch, old Italian, Provençal, Basque, Burgundian, and patois carols the editor has been fortunate enough to obtain the help of experts who have furnished him with literal translations. From these the librettists have composed their verses. Readers may therefore be assured that in this collection they will find no 'faked' English texts. The widest latitude must necessarily be allowed to librettists in their methods of expression, but whether the verses in this collection are literal translations or free paraphrases, there will at least be found in them nothing contrary to the originals.

EXAMPLE 1

96 **In middle winter they set out**
(Belenen sortu zaigu)

Old Basque carol. Words Tr. by Rev. J. O'Connor.

2. 'Now Mary his espoused wife was nigh
The time of her unburdening:
O'ershadow'd by the power of the Most High
To Bethlehem she bore a King.
Yet at the close of her most heavy day
No room she found her head to lay.

3. Quirinus' first enrolling was in peace,
   And all the town was at carouse:
   So no one could a little chamber lease
   A childing woman for to house
   Saint Joseph weeping, sought again the wild
   And there she laid her only child.

4. Did ever joy and sorrow nearer blend?
   'Twas in this grief our joy began,
   Triumphant joy whose day shall never end
   When God became the Son of Man
   And every generation calls her blest
   From whose ill-ease came forth our rest.

We can hope that some publisher will reprint Richard Terry's *Two Hundred Folk Carols*. Meanwhile, choral conductors who can find copies in libraries or through out-of-print book dealers have ready-made carol service music available to them. Why not have a whole service of Italian carols or of Basque carols? The music in this collection is easily adaptable to four-part choral performance or to unison singing. What could be more comforting to the harried choral conductor with too much music to prepare and too little rehearsal time than to be working on lovely carols which, if part-learning time runs out, can be sung in unison, with or without accompaniment.

EXAMPLE 2

80   The Gouty Carol
          (Li a proun de gent)

Provencal Noël. Words Tr. by the Rev. J. O'Connor.

The words of this carol would appear to have been highly popular judging by the number of tunes with which they are associated. No less than four are in Saboly's collection. [*Ed.*]

2. Shepherds awake
   Out there upon the mountain
   Shepherds awake
   Have seen a messenger.
   He cried them: Ware!
   Go over to the Valley.
   He cried them: Ware!
   The Son of God is born!
      My leg is aching worse! etc.

3. Yon hefty brutes
   That go a-caterwauling
   Take off their boots
   And pad it fair and soft.
   If I catch up,
   (They turn, they hear me bawling)
   When I catch up
   I'll give 'em fair and soft.
      My leg is aching worse! etc.

4. Horse, you're a screw,
   Not worth the five brass pennies
   I gave for you
   Last Martinmas's fair.
   If you ate road
   As well as you eat fodder
   Ho! If you could
   I'd ride you to the war!
      My leg is aching worse! etc.

5. When I have seen
   The Son of God the Father,
   When I have seen
   The King of Paradise,
   And when I have been
   And hail'd His virgin-mother
   Look you! this pain
   Will vanish in a trice.
      My leg is aching worse! etc.

EXAMPLE 3

126   The world has waited long

Popular Dutch melody of the seventeenth century.
Words written for it by the Rev. Canon John Gray.

2. The shepherds came to seek
   The Babe unlike another.
   They never saw so meek
   A maiden and a mother;
   For Mary never stirred,
   So still her vigil keeping

While God's eternal Word
Was in the manger sleeping.
Sing, Alleluia! (*bis.*)

3. While men and beasts and birds
Were sunk in sleep or drowsing,
And while the flocks and herds
Were on the mountains browsing,
In heaven and on earth
Were choirs and angels singing
The noble Saviour's birth,
All peace and blessing bringing.
Sing Alleluia! (*bis.*)

Obscure Carol Classics III:
Publications of the Carol Society

William E. Studwell
Dorothy Jones

I. HISTORICAL BACKGROUND

By William E. Studwell

The Carol Society "was founded at New Haven, Connecticut, December, 1923, to 'recover, publish, or circulate old Christmas carols and to encourage carol singing.' "[1] The Society apparently ended around 1947, when the last of the nineteen volumes of carols, which it issued during its existence, was published. The reason for its demise, which is less certain than the reason for its founding, seems to have been the death of Edward Bliss Reed (1872-1940) of Yale University, Secretary of the Carol Society, and the prime mover of this short-lived organization. Despite its relatively brief tenure, the Society contributed significantly to its stated purpose, for the *Publications of the Carol Society* collectively are one of the most valuable bodies of material on Christmas carols ever produced.

Starting in 1924 and until 1939, the Society issued annual collections of eight carols (typically 36 pages). No volume was issued in 1940, apparently due to Reed's death, but the work continued for a while after, with volumes being published in 1941, 1942, and 1947. From the first to the sixteenth volume, the series was published by Stainer & Bell, London,

William E. Studwell and Dorothy Jones, "Obscure Carol Classics III: *Publications of the Carol Society*," *Choral Journal* 29 (October 1988): 5-8. © 1988 by the American Choral Directors Association, P.O. Box 6310, Lawton, Oklahoma 73506-0310. U.S.A. Used by permission.

with musical arrangements by David Stanley Smith and English translations and very good historical notes by Reed. Volumes 17, 18, 19 were
published by Galaxy Music Corporation, New York, with musical arrangements by Luther M. Noss (vol. 17 & 18) and Marshall Bartholomew (vol.
19), and translations and notes by Alfred Raymond Bellinger.

The series is of very high quality in scholarship and artistic taste and
has put into print a large number of folk carols (152) from a variety of
cultures. As a whole, the songs are found in few other places if at all. The
titles in the series are:

1. Eight Traditional French Noels
2. Eight Traditional Christmas Carols
3. Old French and Franconian Carols
4. Old French and German Carols
5. Old Christmas Carols
6. Traditional Christmas Carols
7. Old French and Polish Carols
8. Old French and Czecho-Slovakian Christmas Carols
9. Traditional Basque and Flemish Christmas Carols
10. Russian, Basque, and Flemish Carols
11. Swiss, English, and Swedish Carols
12. Provençal and Russian Carols
13. Eight Old Christmas Carols
14. Old Carols for Christmas
15. Flemish and Other Christmas Carols
16. Provençal and Other Christmas Carols
17. Eight Swiss and French Carols
18. Eight French and Flemish Carols
19. Eight Burgundian Carols

From this list, it is quite easy to receive the correct impression that
Publications of the Carol Society is not everyday or routine fare among the
literature of Christmas carols. Very much living up to its credo, the Society
has produced an exceptionally fine and worthwhile group of publications.
Unfortunately, because of the limited distribution of the series, this multi-
volume mini-masterpiece has not received the attention it deserves.

II: COMMENTARY ON THE MUSIC

By Dorothy Jones

Three of the volumes of the Carol Society Publications have been
chosen for comment. The kind of information given about the carols, and
the format of the publication is similar in all of the volumes.

Old French and Polish Carols, Vol. 7, is a collection of five Old French and three Polish carols. As in the other volumes of the Publications, the sources of each carol are given in the preface. The carols are here arranged for four-part mixed choir, and are intended for practiced performance rather than group singing. Each voice part has a separate staff above the accompaniment.

The Polish carol, "I Hasten Early" is musically interesting, with a rhythm that is slightly agitated but, at the same time, rocks like a lullaby. The D major brightness of the first two measures of the carol slips quickly into the more poignant G minor, the key in which the carol is set. Both rhythm and key add to the mood variations of this carol. The fact that the translated words do not fit the music as well as do the words of most of the other carols is explained in the source note (preface, p. 3): "The Polish metre for this carol is so rich in its many rhymes that it could not be imitated without altering greatly the meaning, and accordingly all rhymes are omitted in the translation" (Example 1).

Swiss, English, and Swedish Carols, Volume 11, contains several very appealing carol-anthems. The Swiss carol "Christmas Eve Dream" is a serene piece with charming story-words. The first three verses are:

> On Christmas eve I fell asleep (So still it was) in slumbers deep.
> Great joy that sleep discloses.
> My soul found sweetness greater far
> than honey or sweet roses,
> Than honey or sweet roses.
>
> I dreamt to me an angel came who
> led me on to Bethlehem,
> To far Judea going.
> What there befell to you I tell, a
> marvel to you showing,
> A marvel to you showing.
>
> I entered in a stable where the ox
> and ass from manger there
> Were feeding, while beside them
> An old man and a maiden mourned
> (such sorrow did betide them,
> Such sorrow did betide them.)

The tranquillity of the melody is enhanced by the constant repetition of the ♩♩ rhythm in the two identical phrases of which the song consists. The rhythmic retardation at the end of each phrase (♩. |♩) adds to the feeling of restfulness (Example 2).

EXAMPLE 1

6. I HASTEN EARLY

EXAMPLE 2

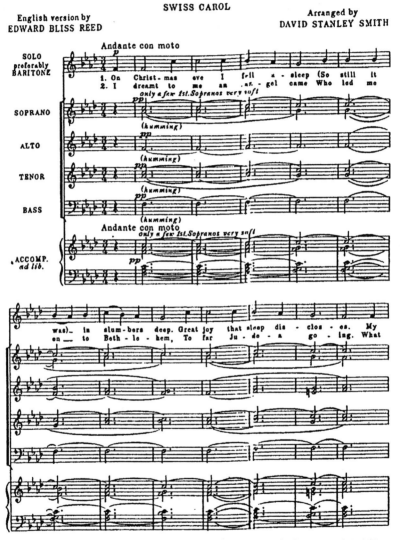

Copyright, 1934, by Stainer & Bell Ltd., 58, Berners Street, London.W.1

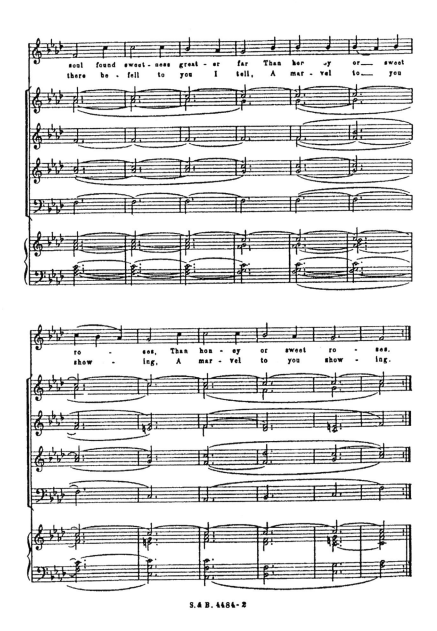

EXAMPLE 3

8. RISE, O DAVID
RUSSIAN CAROL

English version by
N.V. and E.B.R.

Arranged by
DAVID STANLEY SMITH

MADE IN ENGLAND
S. & B. 4368 - 8

The whole carol, found in Karl Simrock's *Deutsche Weihnachtslieder* (Leipzig, 1865) has thirty-five stanzas, of which seven are translated here. David Stanley Smith's arrangements are usually simple and easy enough for the average church choir to learn. This piece is no exception, and its simplicity does not detract from the diversion of the singer or the pleasure of the listener.

Provençal and Russian Carols, Volume 12, contains eight carol anthems. Six of these are Provençal carols from the sixteenth and seventeenth centuries. Five of these carols or noels were among fifty-two noels found in MS 4.485, Bibliothèque d'Avignon, written between 1570 and 1610 and published by J. Clamon and P. Pansier in 1925. Clamon and Pansier wrote in their preface that these noels "were composed by the minor personnel of the Chapter of Notre-Dame des Doms of Avignon–choir directors, organists, instrumentalists, choir singers . . . . Usually these noels were written in two parts–the soprano, taken by the choir boys, and the bass, taken by the men . . . As was the custom, the words of many of these noels were set to popular melodies of the day–marches, dances, slumber songs . . . Some of these noels mention instruments to be played while these songs were sung–flutes, bagpipes, flageolets, oboes, violins. . ." (preface, p. 2).

There are only two Russian carol-anthems in the collection. The carol, "Rise, O David," from an eighteenth-century manuscript (preface, p. 3), is a particularly nice find. There are three musical themes in the carol tune, each sung twice during the course of the anthem. The first, in 2/4 time, which is very sparely harmonized, is followed by a section in 3/8 time. This little section gives the effect of an interlude of bells by using sing-song words and a repetitive melody contained within a very small range of notes. The third section sounds like an announcement, chorded and square. All three parts blend neatly together for a different sort of carol-anthem (Example 3).

NOTE

1. *Swiss, English, and Swedish Carols.* Arranged by David Stanley Smith. London: Stainer & Bell, 1934, p. 2. (Publications of the Carol Society; vol. 11)

THE CHRISTMAS CAROL
AS A CULTURAL PHENOMENON

The Christmas Carol
as a Cultural Phenomenon:
Four Musings on the Music
of the December Holiday

William E. Studwell

Christmas comes every year whether or not we are prepared for it, or want it to, and the music of Christmas is a constant, inevitable, and culturally enormous companion to the holiday. Whether we become lovingly immersed in the music or just tolerate it or even despise it, Western society cannot escape it. Christmas music is in so many places so much of the time during the holiday season.

Yet the cultural role of Christmas music is at best only fuzzily or partially understood. Anyone who thinks much about the phenomenon would probably come up with the impression that Christmas music is a significant component of our civilization, but probably would be hazy about the reasons for or the details of this concept.

To help clarify and amplify the situation, four major considerations relating to the cultural forces created by Christmas music, more specifically, the carol, will be examined. Although these four aspects can be viewed and analyzed as separate and distinct entities, it should not be forgotten that the four are closely affiliated and even intertwined like the holly and the ivy in the famous English folk carol.

From *The Hymn* (Vol. 45, No. 4, October 1994). Copyright (c) 1994 by The Hymn Society in the United States and Canada. Used by permission.

[Haworth co-indexing entry note]: "The Christmas Carol as a Cultural Phenomenon: Four Musings on the Music of the December Holiday." Studwell, William E. Co-published simultaneously in *Music Reference Services Quarterly* (The Haworth Press, Inc.) Vol. 6, No. 4, 1998, pp. 137-145; and: *Publishing Glad Tidings: Essays on Christmas Music* (William E. Studwell, and Dorothy E. Jones) The Haworth Press, Inc., 1998, pp. 137-145. Single or multiple copies of this article are available for a fee from The Haworth Document Delivery Service [1-800-342-9678, 9:00 a.m. - 5:00 p.m. (EST). E-mail address: getinfo@haworth.com].

CONSIDERATION 1

Christmas Is a Strange Holiday

There can be no doubt that Christmas is a strange, curious, or contradictory holiday. It is an odd mixture of sacred and secular ingredients. Sometimes this blend of religious and nonreligious elements results in such a hodgepodge that the sacred cannot clearly be distinguished from the secular. The typical Christmas tree, a key secular manifestation, is decorated with sacred symbols like angels and stars as well as secular symbols like snowmen and reindeer. Santas and manger scenes are often adjacent or even intermixed. (In the United States, it should be noted, such curious combinations are more than occasionally dictated by court decisions relating to the separation of church and state.) And perhaps the strangest bedfellows are the various sacred and secular holiday songs which are routinely grouped together on recordings, on radio and television, and in carol singing. It is not rare to have "Jingle Bells" and "Joy to the World," for example, performed on the same occasion. Such co-existence is not necessarily incompatible, for the psychological joys of the holiday as expressed in even the most secular songs can be complementary to the spiritual joys of Christmas.[1]

This holiday mix of sacred and secular is not just a characteristic of late-twentieth-century North America. Anyone who has read Charles Dickens' 1843 masterpiece *A Christmas Carol* understands that London of a century and a half ago celebrated Christmases with a similar pattern.[2] Even the carol of *A Christmas Carol*, which is inflicted upon Scrooge in the first part of the story, is a muddle of both secular and sacred facets. "God Rest You Merry, Gentlemen" is a completely religious song, but the lively tune and frequent misinterpretation of the words "Merry Gentlemen" in the title has created a misimpression that the song is secular.[3]

On top of the common and even routine blending of religious and nonreligious, the length of the holiday season is debatable. Technically, Christmas is only a single day, December the 25th. In reality, however, the season in the United States stretches from at least Thanksgiving to as late as February. The secular side of the season, notably the commercial component, comes into full bloom the Friday after Thanksgiving. In fact, a few years ago a trip to the most famous department store in Chicago on Columbus Day (October 12th) gave this author the opportunity to witness Christmas decorations prominently displayed weeks prior to Halloween. That is, the Christmas season was being activated two holidays and two months before Christmas Day.

The sacred side of the season, specifically the liturgical calendars followed by some denominations, allows for the observance of the season as late as February. You can imagine the shock experienced by this author, raised in the Baptist tradition, when he first sang "We Three Kings" in early February as part of the celebration of Epiphany in a Methodist church. And it should be noted that although American society extends the season longer than any other culture, sacred and secular traditions in other western countries also result in very long holiday observances there.

We are more or less aware of the cohabitation and conflict relationship between sacred and secular in the celebration of Christmas with its adjacent events and the length of the holiday season. These two factors indicate that Christmas is a major influence on Western society for at least a month every year. Few, if any, societal aspects totally escape the wide and deep cultural reaches of the holiday. With both the Christian church and everyday life so significantly involved with the holiday season, the observance of Christmas and its adjacent events is, without doubt, the most important single phenonemon in the Western calendar. By obvious extension, the large body of song which permeates December and to a much lesser degree the rest of the long season has to be the most important single group contributing to the yearly functioning of Western society.

CONSIDERATION 2

Christmas Carols Are a Mass Phenomenon

The Christmas carol has been defined in various and sometimes quite contradictory ways over the years. However, it should be pointed out that the three books which arguably are the most important volumes in twentieth-century carol literature do have some definite areas of agreement. The most important collection of carols, *The Oxford Book of Carols*, which was published in 1928 and reissued in 1964, describes the carol as follows:

> Carols are songs with a religious impulse that are simple, hilarious, popular, and modern. . . . The typical carol gives voice to the common emotions of healthy people in language that can be understood and music that can be shared by all.[4]

The somewhat puzzling usage of the term "modern" in the above passage is subsequently clarified:

> Carols, moreover, were always modern, expressing the manner in which the ordinary man at his best understood the ideas of his age.[5]

The most important history of and commentary on carols, Erik Routley's *The English Carol* (1958), which despite its title also significantly
covers the carol in general, observes that carols are "not remote dogma but
a texture of life . . . something like a 'general dance.'"[6]

The most important reference work on carols, William Studwell's
Christmas Carols: A Reference Guide (1985), gives the carol the following
very broad definition:

> A song used to celebrate Christmas and its adjacent events (includ-
> ing Advent, Epiphany, the New Year, and to some extent the winter
> season).[7]

This definition is immediately followed by the explanation that:

> One of the more important characteristics of the carol is its long-term
> and widespread mass appeal. It is a phenomenon popular with di-
> verse and varied segments of society. . . . The carol is meant to be
> actively sung, played, and heard, year after year, by all types of
> persons.[8]

These three descriptions of the carol, published with an interval of
about a generation between each of them (1928, 1958, and 1985), all
portray the carol with broad strokes. Furthermore, they all make note that
the carol is a mass phenomenon. Percy Dearmer, in *The Oxford Book*, uses
the terms and phrases "ordinary man, "popular," "common emotions,"
"language that can be understood," and "music that can be shared by all."
Erik Routley uses the colorful expressions "texture of life" and "general
dance." Studwell uses the phrases "widespread mass appeal," "phenomenon popular with diverse and varied segments of society," and "all types
of persons."

One of the causes of this mass phenomenon is, as discussed above, the
nature of Christmas as a holiday which encompasses both the sacred and
secular portions of our lives. Another major factor contributing to the
phenomenon is that carols have not as a whole emanated from well-known
artists, and on those occasions when they did, the songs were usually
minor or irregular or tangential products of their artistic activities. With a
few exceptions, famous persons have not deliberately set out to create
Christmas songs. Throughout history the carol has been regarded as a
minor genre with a lower social status, although in the twentieth century,
the financial rewards of Christmas song writing can be tremendous.

In other words, the carol is "in general the domain of the obscure."[9]
The vast majority of carols are anonymous, or from folk sources, or are the

most important artistic creation of little known persons. To further emphasize the extent and scope of this mass phenomenon, in addition, there is the curious "Jewish connection" to some of the more renowned Christmas songs. The music for "Hark! The Herald Angels Sing" is from an 1840 non-Christmas work by the German master Felix Mendelssohn, whose grandfather was a prominent Jew. French composer Adolphe Adam, who created the 1847 melody for "Cantique de Noël" ("O Holy Night") because of a request from a friend, was Jewish. Eddie Cantor, the famous American Jewish entertainer, was the first person to sing "Santa Claus Is Comin' to Town" (on his radio program in 1934). And the fabulous Irving Berlin, a Jew, wrote the immensely popular "White Christmas" for the movie "Holiday Inn" (1942).

To summarize, one does not have to be famous or even a Christian to create a successful Christmas song. The carol is truly a mass phenomenon, and, to paraphrase Karl Marx, is in some ways a bit of musical opiate for the masses during December. While Marx's effort to eradicate religion, his alleged opiate of the masses, by means of Communism has failed miserably, Christmas music continues to satisfy and stimulate the masses and is expected to do so for a long time.

CONSIDERATION 3

Christmas Carols Have Flourished More Outside the Church Than in the Church

The carol and the church have not been constant and close companions throughout history. Until the late Medieval period, all known Christmas songs were Latin or Greek hymns. Around 1400 in England, and somewhat earlier on the European continent, dance carols which were popular with the common people began to appear. Some of these songs were secular and some had religious content, but none of them were allowed in English or American church services until at least the late nineteenth century. In fact, it wasn't until recent decades that some of the finest religious carols, for example, "God Rest You Merry, Gentlemen" and "Go Tell It on the Mountain" could be found in many hymnals. In part, this exclusion was because of the lively tone of such songs, and in part it was because of the nonecclesiastical origins of the songs.

Even the more standard and conservative hymn carols suffered exclusion from churches for various reasons at various times. German Protestant churches after the beginning of the Reformation, for instance, tended to exclude or at least downplay carols of Catholic origin. In England the carol was de-emphasized in churches for about two centuries after the Puritan suppression of the celebration of Christmas in the 1640s.

One of the observers of this situation in England was the famous carol collector William Sandys, who in 1833 commented,

> In many parts of the kingdom, especially in the northern and western parts, this festival is still kept up with spirit among the middling and lower classes, though its influence is on the wane even with them; the genius of the present age requires work and not play.[10]

(It should be noted that the reason for the decline of Christmas was not just the lingering effects of the Puritans but also the major social and economic upheavals created by the Industrial Revolution, which had begun in the second half of the eighteenth century.) Not only did Sandys observe that the celebration of the holiday had fallen on hard times, but in addition his statement suggests strongly that the main support for the continuance of the celebration came from the common people, not organized religion. The church, of course, had never abandoned the most basic sacred aspects of Christmas, but anything resembling festive observances was not a strong part of the church.

By the middle of the nineteenth century, however, both secular and sacred forces were altering the situation. On the secular front, Charles Dickens's classic, *A Christmas Carol*, was an enormous impetus to the increasing of the awareness of and appreciation for the December holiday. As a recent author commented, "Dickens has even been credited with almost single-handedly reviving the holiday customs."[11] At about the same time, "the new movement in the church was causing some of the young high-church parsons to think wistfully about carols."[12] In 1868 an important carol collector, William Henry Husk, said that " 'a certain section of the clergy' had made attempts to revive a taste for the use of Christmas carols amongst their parishioners."[13]

Before the end of the century, the carol had sufficiently returned to church services in England that the carol collector Richard Robert Chope could happily observe,

> It has been an arduous, prolonged and costly work to restore the use of carols in Divine Service, and thus make into an act of worship what was well-nigh considered only as a recreation at a social gathering. But now they . . . have begun to love the old, old story and grow familiar with the carol-strain at Christmas and Epiphany.[14]

Chope's statement, though directed toward one country in one specific period, is a summary of the dilemma of the historical relationship of the carol and the church. That is, secular carols need not apply for admittance, and sacred carols could only be admitted into the church environment at certain times and under certain conditions. This fragile and sporadic relationship of the carol and the church is closely affiliated with the tendency of the carol to be a mass phenomenon, existing, in large part, at some distance from society's most mainstream and official establishments.

CONSIDERATION 4

Christmas Carols Are Probably the Most Influential Body of Songs in the Western World

In discussing the previous three considerations, some facets of the cultural impact of the carol were touched upon. The very strong presence of the carol for roughly a month each year and the carol as a mass phenomenon popular with all segments of society suggest that the lowly carol is indeed quite influential. Add to these two concepts two other factors, and there is a very strong case for the Christmas carol being the most culturally dominant body of enduring or lasting songs in Western society.[15]

One, all other possible rivals fall short in some way. Popular songs, by their very definition, are largely excluded. National and patriotic songs are very influential in their own countries, but have little impact elsewhere. Religious songs in general transcend national boundaries, but even within Christianity a large proportion of them tend to be sectarian and tend to be important to only certain groups. Furthermore, as a whole only the religious are affected by them, and church goers can also be quite sporadic in their interest in church. Folk songs can be international, but only have a strong cultural influence in their home areas. In addition, folk songs have a tendency to not cross class lines. One other category, songs from classical or serious music, are not particularly influential with the average person, although they are performed throughout the world. In contrast, carols are international in influence and affect all classes and virtually all groups in society. And they don't affect just Western society. There are many Christians in Asia, Africa, and the Pacific. Furthermore, carols sometimes can be found in non-Christian areas of life. For instance, during a television story a few years ago about a Tokyo department store decorated for Christmas, one could distinctly hear in the background the glorious strains of "Hark! The Herald Angels Sing."

Two, in spite of their extensive worldwide appeal and cultural impact, the number of important or famous carols number only in the dozens, compared with hundreds or more in some of the other categories of songs. The average American, for example, is probably familiar with about fifty or so Christmas songs. The relatively small number of important or widely known carols makes the very sizeable cultural impact of the carol even more notable. One test of this "small yet sizable" concept would be to write a highly successful and internationally renowned Christmas song. Even if the song creator did nothing else that gained attention, the person would probably be remembered in history. This path to lasting fame is also true for writing a national anthem, but the fame in such a situation would mostly be confined within one country.

As a personal aside, this author has made almost two-hundred media appearances relating to songs. Although some stories about college songs, patriotic songs, etc., have garnered considerable national attention, the annual stories done about Christmas songs have for almost a decade been the most consistent in catching the attention of the public. There is no doubt that the reason for this sustained interest is the subject matter–the Christmas carol!

All these factors strongly point toward Christmas carols being the most influential group of enduring songs in Western society. Given the purpose and nature of Christmas, we should all be delighted that no other body of songs affects us as much as the common and familiar Christmas carol. Long live the carol!

NOTES

1. For an essay on this concept, see William E. Studwell, "Deck the Halls with Boughs of Holly: The Role of the Jolly Secular Carol in a Religious Holiday," *The American Organist* 23: 11 (Nov. 1989), pp. 101-102.

2. For a very good annotated edition of the Dickens book, see *The Annotated Christmas Carol* (New York: C.N. Potter, 1976).

3. For a commentary on this carol, Dickens' *A Christmas Carol*, and the interweaving of sacred and secular, see William E. Studwell, "A Dickens Tale: The Story of a Christmas Carol," *Journal of Church Music* 24: 10 (Dec. 1982), pp. 5-8.

4. Percy Dearmer, Ralph Vaughan Williams, and Martin Shaw, eds., *The Oxford Book of Carols*, (London: Oxford University Press, 1928), p. v.

5. Ibid, p. vi.

6. Erik Routley, *The English Carol* (London: H. Jenkins, 1958), p. 242.

7. William E. Studwell, *Christmas Carols: A Reference Guide* (New York: Garland, 1985) p. xi.

8. Ibid.

9. Ibid.

10. William Sandys, *Christmas Carols, Ancient and Modern* (London: R. Beckley, 1833), p. 1.

11. Michael Hearn, in the introduction to *The Annotated Christmas Carol*, (p. 1). See note 2.

12. *The Oxford Book of Carols*, p. xii.

13. Ibid, p. xiii.

14. Quoted in Routley, p. 182.

15. For an essay on this concept, see William E. Studwell, "The Cultural Impact of the Christmas Carol," *Journal of Church Music* 24: 10 (Dec. 1982), pp. 13-14.

The Christmas Carol:
A Bibliographic Essay

Dorothy E. Jones

The literature on the history of the Christmas carol as a musical genre of cultural and theological significance is replete with questions, debates, and opinions as well as with many stories and myths. While the list of scholarly literature about Christmas carols is not extensive, a few serious studies of carols have been written which treat the history and character of all kinds of carols, but discuss Christmas carols at greater length than any other kind of carol.

This essay is limited to selected books which are written in the English language and which (a) are about the origin and development of the genre "carols" or (b) are historically prominent collections of carols which are sung in English-speaking cultures and which are accompanied by narrative text, or (c) are useful reference books on carols. The publications included in the bibliography are all readily available through libraries with good interlibrary loan services.

It is very interesting to compare the opinions of various researchers concerning the definition of a "carol." Are carols firmly or exclusively rooted in ancient dancing songs? Are they rooted in minstrelsy or monastery, in orally-transmitted folk tunes or in words and music composed for a purpose? The definition and the origin are inextricably entwined and have been a matter of differing opinions for many years. Carols may, liberally defined, spring from any or all of the disputed roots. However, they seem to have transcended the barriers of limited audience which segregate most types of music, and have become songs loved by huge and disparate

[Haworth co-indexing entry note]: "The Christmas Carol: A Bibliographic Essay." Jones, Dorothy E. Co-published simultaneously in *Music Reference Services Quarterly* (The Haworth Press, Inc.) Vol. 6, No. 4, 1998, pp. 147-152; and: *Publishing Glad Tidings: Essays on Christmas Music* (William E. Studwell, and Dorothy E. Jones) The Haworth Press, Inc., 1998, pp. 147-152. Single or multiple copies of this article are available for a fee from The Haworth Document Delivery Service [1-800-342-9678, 9:00 a.m. - 5:00 p.m. (EST). E-mail address: getinfo@haworth.com].

groups of people all over the world. It is enlightening and enjoyable to read scholars' explorations and speculations about the beginnings of carol-singing. As soon as one moves beyond the carol sung by the angels to the shepherds, as recorded in the Bible, one encounters informed guesses and varied opinions concerning the definition, origin and history of carols.

Edmondstoune Duncan's book, *The Story of the Carol* (London: The Walter Scott Publishing Co., Ltd., 1911) is one of the early books on the history of the carol. There is a wealth of information in this book. However, though the content is certainly erudite, the narrative jumps from century to century and the reader is likely to become entangled and confused. Eric Routley, in *The English Carol* (New York: Oxford University Press, 1959), notes that Duncan's book was "written at a time when certain theories about the origin of the carol were current which are now seriously doubted, and when modern conventions of scholarship governing the transcription of ancient music had not yet become fully established" (p. 18). Nevertheless, Duncan's descriptions of the carol in Greek and Roman celebrations, early ecclesiastical services, medieval plays and what he calls "strange ceremonies" are valuable. Duncan writes: "As early as the year 129, say the French historians, Telesphorus, Bishop of Rome, instituted the custom of celebrating the Nativity with songs of Noel, or Christmas carols" (p. 11). S. Baring-Gould, in his Introduction to Richard Chope's *Carols for Use in the Church* (London: William Clower & Sons, Ltd., 1894a) and William J. Phillips, in his *Carols: Their Origin, Music, and Connection with Mystery Plays* (London: George Routledge and Sons Ltd., 1921) discuss "first carols" in conjunction with St. Francis in the 13th century. St. Francis originated creches and carols in local churches as a way to teach the Bible story to people who could not read. The representations inspired the singing of carols. However, Dr. Phillips' book emphasizes the secular and popular strand of carol history, with a chapter on "Carols and Dancing" and another on "Mystery-Plays." He shows how carols were used for teaching and enjoyed as entertainment. He discusses several story-telling carols, numeral carols, and wassail songs.

The Early English Carols edited by Richard Leighton Greene (Oxford: Clarendon Press, 1935) presents to us the lyrics of 474 carols, most of them edited from original sources or from rotograph copies located at Huntington Library. The 26-page bibliography of original sources, as well as the 98-page section of notes on individual carols are gold mines for the music scholar. The first 145 pages of the book, called the Introduction but divided into 6 chapters, includes a fine explication of the relationship of the carol to dance, ballad, hymn, antiphon and other musical and poetic forms, all set carefully into the sociohistoric picture. A later book by

Greene, *A Selection of English Carols* (Oxford: Clarendon Press, 1962) is partially an abridgement of *The Early English Carols*, but contains a new introduction, some carols discovered in the British Museum MS. Egerton 3307, and new information on the provenance of some of the carols.

Christmas Carols Printed in the Sixteenth Century, edited by Edward Bliss Reed (Cambridge, MA: Harvard University Press, 1932) includes facsimiles of Kele's *Christmas Carolles Newely Inprynted*, found, after a long disappearance, in the Huntington Library, and facsimiles of other carols from the Bodleian and the British Museum. Reed provided the book with a very interesting 42-page introduction. In his discussion of the emergence of the carol, for example, he says he believes that there was "no question of sanctifying profane song for pious uses; it was rather the opposite process–in the noels and carols, songs of the church were secularized" (p. xxiii). Reed's detailed description of the travels, disappearance and rediscovery of Kele's collection of carols is invaluable since this collection is considered by many to be the most important printed collection of English 16th-century carols that we have.

Four other carol books should be noted because they are collections of hard-to-find carols and include explanatory text. *A Medieval Carol Book*, edited by Sir Richard R. Terry (London: Burns Oates and Washbourne Ltd., [1932]) is a collection of carols from the Bodleian Library, Oxford, the Library of Trinity College, Cambridge, and The British Museum, with one from the *Dominican Graduale*. Because it was intended for practical use, Terry added vocal parts to the carols for better performance. The preface contains an in-depth discussion of the medieval carol as compared to those carols which grew out of the late 19th century revival. In *Two Hundred Folk Carols* (London: Burns Oates and Washbourne, 1933), R. Terry gathered sacred and secular carols from all over Europe. *A Garland of Christmas Carols, Ancient and Modern*, edited with notes by Joshua Sylvester (London: John Camden Hotton, 1861) is a lovely collection of 74 carol texts. The title page declares that this collection includes "some never before given in any collection." The Introduction includes several historical vignettes and a complete handbill for one of the miracle plays. Eclectic remarks prefixed to each carol include notes about the author, explanations of archaic words, and settings. Edith Rickert's *Ancient English Christmas Carols MCCC to MDCC* (London: Chatto & Windus, 1928) has a valuable Introduction.

The Oxford Book of Carols (London: Oxford University Press, 1928) compiled and edited by Percy Dearmer, R. Vaughan Williams and Martin Shaw, is a classic collection which is still a staple of present-day choral conductors. Percy Dearmer's definition of "carol" in the Preface to the collection is probably the most quoted definition of our time. He says, "Carols are songs with a religious impulse that are simple, hilarious, popular, and modern." The definition needs Dearmer's explanation of "hilarious" and "modern" to be understood properly. The collection is closely bound to Dearmer's definition of the carol. It is a most wonderful collection of Easter, spring, harvest and a multitude of other kinds of carols, with Advent and Christmas carols being the most numerous. The authors revised *The Oxford Book of Carols* in 1964, adding original words for translated carols and updating notes and references to include information from Greene's *The Early English Carols*.

There is a small carol book, *The Penguin Book of Christmas Carols*, compiled, edited, and annotated by Elizabeth Poston (Harmondsworth, England; Baltimore: Penguin Books, 1965), which is related to *The Oxford Book of Carols* in an odd sort of way. Elizabeth Poston's mission, as described in her Introduction, seems to be the correction of distortions and errors which occurred during the Anglican revival of carols in the nineteenth century. Ms. Poston was asked by Ralph Vaughan Williams to join him in revising the contents of *The Oxford Book of Carols*. Williams died before this was accomplished, and Poston's carol book is, in her words, "a start towards the heart of the matter in a collection of carols for practical use with translations and English versions, where these are needed, nearer to the meaning and spirit of the originals than those they replace" (p. 17). The notes on the carols are a superb resource.

Christmas and Its Carols by Reginald Nettel (London: The Faith Press, 1960) is a small book published shortly before Poston's carol book. Like Poston, Nettel has ideas that conflict with those of other researchers. His book is written with much conviction and with distinctive style. Fascinating stories and myths related to the development of the carol as well as perceptive views on the nature and influence of some of England's holy days and festivals abound. Both casual reader and scholar will react to such challenging comments as:

> It has been said that in the time of the English Commonwealth in the seventeenth century the waits were disbanded. This is just another way of painting the Puritans blacker than they were, and shows quite remarkable lack of understanding; the Puritans were not opposed to all music and entertainment, and the waits were neither pagan nor papist–why should the Puritans disband them? They did not. (p. 69)

or

> A final warning should be given not to deal uncharitably with popular misconceptions. Any imaginative work can be rendered dubious by intellectual questioning. (p. 138)

Musica Britannica (London: Stainer & Bell, 1951-) and *The New Grove Dictionary of Music and Musicians* (London: Macmillan Publishers Ltd., 1980) offer us concise, learned and orderly discourse on carols. However, if I wanted to read only one book about carols, I would choose Erik Routley's *The English Carol* (New York: Oxford University Press, 1959). Routley obviously enjoys his subject matter and exudes a happy combination of humility and confidence in dealing with it. He writes: "My purpose is to tell the story of the carol, which story I owe entirely to the learned writers and researchers whom I am about to name; but as the story unfolds itself I hope to show what comment it offers on the developing social and religious life of our country over a period of half a thousand years" (Introduction, p. 17). His chapters embrace medieval manuscript carols, ballads, medieval plays, carols of the Puritan period, Christmas hymns, carols brought to us from other countries and contemporary carols, all presented in an enthusiastic but scholarly manner.

We have not been without scholars writing about carols during the last 2 decades. Adrienne F. Block's fine 2-volume set, *The Early French Parody Noel* (Ann Arbor, Michigan: UMI Research Press, c 1983) does not fall within the scope of this bibliography, but Volume 1 has an excellent chapter, "The Background and Precursors of the Noel," which explores the roots of carols. There is a particularly interesting section on why and how the secular and sacred flowed together, contaminating or enriching each other, during the middle ages.

William W. Utterback's master's thesis, "A Study of Five Religious Christmas Carols from *The Oxford Book of Carols*" (Kirksville, Missouri: Northeast Missouri State University, 1985) is a study of 5 carols which he considered unfamiliar but very singable. He aimed at bringing the rich variety of carols available in *The Oxford Book of Carols* to the attention of a wider public. At least one of the five carols he studied, "Mid-Winter," has become more commonly known in recent years and is now included in several major denominational hymnals.

The New Oxford Book of Carols (Oxford: Oxford University Press, c 1992) and *The Shorter New Oxford Book of Carols* (Oxford; New York: Music Dept., Oxford University Press, c 1993) are edited by Hugh Keyte and Andrew Parrott. These are new publications and are not in any way "new editions" of the 1928 *Oxford Book of Carols*, though there is a great deal of overlap. The *New Oxford Book of Carols* contains 201 carols. It offers us a great deal of valuable information pertinent to historians, musicologists and church musicians in the 19-page Introduction, two substantial essays, and extensive notes which follow each carol. The division into "composed" and "traditional" carols is understandable when viewed in conjunction with the editors' definition of the carol. Keyte and Parrott describe Dearmer's definition in *The Oxford Book* as "less a definition than as a manifesto, a declaration of war on all that was convoluted, sanctimonious, esoteric, and quaint in the Christmas repertory of his day" (p. xxii). Because Keyte and Parrott define carols more broadly, they include favorites, such as "Adeste Fideles," which were not included in *The Oxford Book* because they were "hymns." *The New Oxford Book* also includes more carols from America and "composed carols that do not conform to conventional notions of 'correct harmony' " (Appendix 3, p. 669).

William E. Studwell is probably the most prolific and visible literary propagator of the Christmas Carol at the present, with approximately 50 articles and 3 books on carols to his credit. His *Christmas Carols: A Reference Guide* (New York and London: Garland Publishing, Inc., 1985) is "the first reference book in the English language . . . which broadly and comprehensively deals with Christmas carols" (p. ix). Studwell's definition of the Christmas carol is the broadest of all: "A song used to celebrate Christmas and its adjacent events" (p. xi). His is a very large bibliography of carols selected from approximately 150 listed sources. The "Historical Dictionary" which is the body of the book consists of information on the lyrics, music, and sources of 789 carols. A Title Index, Person and Group Index and Place Index make the book useful for program planners and music directors, as well as the naturally curious carol enthusiast. Another of Mr. Studwell's books, *The Christmas Carol Reader* (New York: The Haworth Press, Inc., 1995) is a collection of vignettes on about 140 carols. It can be a read-through book or a reference book.

Index

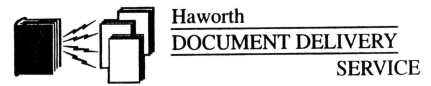

Haworth
DOCUMENT DELIVERY
SERVICE

This valuable service provides a single-article order form for any article from a Haworth journal.

- *Time Saving:* No running around from library to library to find a specific article.
- *Cost Effective:* All costs are kept down to a minimum.
- *Fast Delivery:* Choose from several options, including same-day FAX.
- *No Copyright Hassles:* You will be supplied by the original publisher.
- *Easy Payment:* Choose from several easy payment methods.

Open Accounts Welcome for ...
- Library Interlibrary Loan Departments
- Library Network/Consortia Wishing to Provide Single-Article Services
- Indexing/Abstracting Services with Single Article Provision Services
- Document Provision Brokers and Freelance Information Service Providers

---

MAIL or *FAX* THIS ENTIRE ORDER FORM TO:

Haworth Document Delivery Service
The Haworth Press, Inc.
10 Alice Street
Binghamton, NY 13904-1580

or FAX: 1-800-895-0582
or CALL: 1-800-342-9678
9am-5pm EST

PLEASE SEND ME PHOTOCOPIES OF THE FOLLOWING SINGLE ARTICLES:

1) Journal Title: _____
   Vol/Issue/Year:_____ Starting & Ending Pages:_____
   Article Title:_____
   _____

2) Journal Title: _____
   Vol/Issue/Year:_____ Starting & Ending Pages:_____
   Article Title:_____
   _____

3) Journal Title: _____
   Vol/Issue/Year:_____ Starting & Ending Pages:_____
   Article Title:_____
   _____

4) Journal Title: _____
   Vol/Issue/Year:_____ Starting & Ending Pages:_____
   Article Title:_____
   _____

(See other side for Costs and Payment Information)

COSTS: Please figure your cost to order quality copies of an article.

1. Set-up charge per article: $8.00
    ($8.00 × number of separate articles)   _____

2. Photocopying charge for each article:
                         1-10 pages: $1.00   _____

                         11-19 pages: $3.00   _____

                         20-29 pages: $5.00   _____

                         30+ pages: $2.00/10 pages   _____

3. Flexicover (optional): $2.00/article   _____

4. Postage & Handling: US: $1.00 for the first article/
                         $.50 each additional article   _____

                         Federal Express: $25.00   _____

                         Outside US: $2.00 for first article/
                         $.50 each additional article_____

5. Same-day FAX service: $.35 per page   _____

GRAND TOTAL: _____

METHOD OF PAYMENT: (please check one)

❑ Check enclosed   ❑ Please ship and bill. PO # _____
             (sorry we can ship and bill to bookstores only! All others must pre-pay)

❑ Charge to my credit card: ❑ Visa; ❑ MasterCard; ❑ Discover;
                         ❑ American Express;

Account Number:_____ Expiration date:_____

Signature: ✗_____

Name: _____ Institution: _____

Address: _____

_____

City: _____ State:_____ Zip:_____

Phone Number: _____ FAX Number: _____

MAIL or *FAX* THIS ENTIRE ORDER FORM TO:

Haworth Document Delivery Service	**or FAX: 1-800-895-0582**
The Haworth Press, Inc.	**or CALL: 1-800-342-9678**
10 Alice Street	9am-5pm EST)
Binghamton, NY 13904-1580	